IT'S HARDER IN HEELS:

Essays by Women Lawyers
Achieving Work-Life Balance

IT'S HARDER IN HEELS:

Essays by Women Lawyers
Achieving Work-Life Balance

Jacquelyn Hersh Slotkin &

Samantha Slotkin Goodman

editors and contributors

Happy holidays Ken
Jackie Slotkin

Vandeplas Publishing

UNITED STATES OF AMERICA

Slotkin, Jacquelyn Hersh
Goodman, Samantha Slotkin

It's Harder in Heels:
Essays by Women Lawyers Achieving Work-Life Balance

Published by:

Vandeplas Publishing - July 2007

801 International Parkway, 5th Floor
Lake Mary, FL. 32746 - USA

www.vandeplaspublishing.com

ISBN: 978-1-60042-026-9
Library of Congress Control Number: 2007929997
© Jacquelyn Hersh Slotkin & Samantha Slotkin Goodman 2007

Printed in the United States of America

Acknowledgement

The most pleasant task in preparing this book for publication is thanking all the people who assisted with our project. We invited a select group of special lawyers – all women – to contribute their observations, experiences, wisdom, and thoughtful insights about their personal lives as lawyers. These women are friends, colleagues, former students, academics, jurists, public servants, and practitioners. Some of their essays document the progress women have made in the legal profession. Some share concerns, describe the injustices and inequities they've experienced, record the challenges of juggling career and family, and celebrate the progress of women. We know everyone is very busy, personally and professionally, and we thank all of our authors for their enthusiastic willingness to participate in the project.

For their support, feedback, legal expertise, creative ideas, and constructive comments, we are indebted to special people: Bob Slotkin (best friend, supporter, defender), for reading and commenting on each essay as it arrived, then performing final corrections; Caroline Marodi, my research assistant, for helping us revise and edit the essays; Andrew Goodman, Samantha's best friend and husband, for coming up with yet another great title; Professor Art Campbell for helping to educate us about copyright law and its application to our project; Professor Thomas Barton for giving us information about Vandeplas Publishers; and finally, we appreciate the advice and expertise of our publisher, Anton Von de Plas, for emailing us a contract to publish our book less than two weeks after receiving the proposal and adding the comment, "The essays give a very good example and idea of the life of women in the legal profession and we believe that every person in the legal profession should read it."

Table of Contents

Summary of Contents

"Approaching Life as a Lawyer and a Cop"

Rana Sampson

Rana Sampson had a good job in the New York City Mayor's Office but believed she should help people in crisis; therefore, she opted to become a New York City police officer. From foot beat to patrol car to undercover narcotics officer and then sergeant, she learned the streets, then earned a law degree at Harvard. Using that degree and her policing experiences, her journey continued at a national think tank, as a White House Fellow, and as head of public safety at a university. She is currently an international crime consultant and co-founder of the Center for Problem-Oriented Policing, which is supported by the U.S. Department of Justice.

"Becoming a Lawyer: An Immigrant's Challenge"

Lilia S. Velasquez

Lilia Velasquez documents her struggles coming to the U.S. from Mexico at nineteen, learning English, attending college, law school (while married with children), and choice of specialty (immigration law). She advocates for the rights of immigrants and refugees and is an international human rights advocate for women. She teaches immigration law, gives legal advice on a weekly television show, works with lawyers and judges in Latin America, and has received numerous awards.

"Canary in the Coal Mine"

Whittney Graham-Beard

Whittney Graham-Beard was at the top of her law school class. When she interviewed for a job where she asked about the lack of female attorneys, the partner answered, "Men are less likely to leave to raise a family." As a single women, she worked as an associate in a large, national firm. She left the firm because she was unhappy with the workload and lifestyle, not because of the pressures of marriage and children. There was no time to even think about a social life. Her essay is a warning to the profession to become more humane so that all lawyers are happy and satisfied with practicing law.

"Everything I Needed to Know for Life I Learned in First Grade"

The Honorable Louisa S. Porter

Judge Porter explains her early years and what influenced her decision to become the first person in her family to attend college. After college, she became a reporter in Vietnam and then started a private investigation business. She decided to attend law school when she realized she was doing all the work and her law firm clients were making significantly more money. She became a trial lawyer, active in legal organizations. She obtained a private pilot's license (and owns a four-seater Piper aircraft). In 1990, just as she was about to embark on a new challenge studying space law, she was appointed to the federal bench.

"Evolution of Choice"

Donna D. Melby

Donna Melby describes her "circle of life." Her professional path was inspired by her role model father who died at a young age. She observed her father in trial (where the only women in the courtroom were on the jury); knew her path would lead to the courtroom; completed college while working; joined a law firm as the only woman lawyer. Her hard work, sacrifice, and passion led to great success as a civil jury trial lawyer. In 2005, she was elected the first woman president of the 50-year-old organization, the American Board of Trial Advocates (a position her father would have held thirty years earlier but for his early demise).

"Fields, Courts, and Leaping High"

Stacey R. Preston

Stacey Preston grew up in Los Angeles and loved sports. She suffered a significant injury that ended her gymnastics career. She attended UCLA, no longer an athlete but an avid student, then law school, then practiced law for ten years – but her interest in and dream about work opportunities in intercollegiate athletics continued. She took a leap of faith, left the practice of law, and went to work in Indianapolis for the NCAA, a national organization celebrating the student athlete. In her position as assistant director of brand strategies and events with the NCAA, she utilizes skills she developed as an attorney.

"Fulfilling Your Destiny"

Andrea L. Johnson

Andrea Johnson describes her journey through life to become a fourth generation educator. She was inspired by her special grandmother, a teacher in Nashville, Tennessee, and her family who valued education. Her mother was a teacher and college administrator, and her father was a dentist and board chair of the community college. She went from Howard University to Harvard Law School to a Wall Street firm to entrepreneurship to teaching law where she found she, too, had the gift of teaching. Her focus on technology led her to develop the first distance-learning class at a U.S. law school.

"How Do They Live?"

Ellen J. Dannin

Ellen Dannin's legal career began with a position as a trial attorney for the National Labor Relations Board following her federal judicial clerkship. She was raised by a single mother in poverty in rural Ohio and escaped the misery of her life through books and the support of the public schools. Her childhood helped her to relate to her worker-clients who she describes as "the real heroes of our democracy" and who helped her to be a good trial lawyer, sensitive and self confident, with an unwavering certainty in the rightness of what she was doing. Now she doesn't try cases; she "tries to teach."

"I Never Wanted to Be a Lawyer"

Julia A. Cline

Julia Cline decided to become a lawyer when her husband became a first-year law student. She knew she needed to educate herself to save her marriage. After graduation, she went to work as a litigator for the federal government. She has juggled marriage, children, and a legal career. She sometimes feels guilty, though she realizes she has been given an opportunity and the skills to be a lawyer.

"Latina in Law"

Gloria A. Sandrino

Gloria Sandrino arrived in the U.S. from Cuba in 1967 with her mother, grandmother, and sister. Her early memories of America were filled with blatant racism. Her mother spoke no English but with two Ph.D.s, she knew she could provide a better life for her children. Her mother's education gave them the opportunity for a middle class life. She attended Harvard Law School, was a corporate attorney in a Wall Street firm, and left her firm when the firm decided its clients were not ready for a partner of color. As a professor, she now researches and teaches about issues of race, ethnicity, and gender.

"Learning to Leave It at Work"

Margo L. Lewis

Margo Lewis explains her early decision to become a lawyer as the child of divorce, and the challenges she faced after becoming a lawyer – as a family law sole practitioner with few clients to developing her practice into a four-person firm, to becoming a named partner in a nine lawyer family law firm. She juggles being a single mom to a daughter and son (and missing none of their first-time experiences) with the challenges of a full time practice. Her insight gained from having children of her own translates to representing children in her divorce practice.

"Life in the Ladies' Lane"

Laurie L. Levenson

Laurie Levenson describes her early years with the U.S. Attorney's office, then pregnancy, then demotion to "chief of training." She had another child soon after becoming a professor at Loyola Law School. She became senior faculty, CBS legal commentator, won "professor of the year," was passed over for an endowed chair – the job was a livelihood for men and a hobby for women – then chose to have another child. Now she is attending kindergarten meetings with mothers who were her former students.

"Mediating My Life: Confessions of a 24/7 Law Mom"

Susan B. Share
Susan Share "shares" a picture of her life as a mother of three while trying to squeeze in work time representing a few clients. Between her house, husband (also a lawyer), her children's activities, driving, cooking, cleaning, and laundry, available time is scarce for the legal work. Her law practice gives her intellectual stimulation and a lot of stress but helps her maintain her self-confidence and a foot in the legal door. Her priority is her children, but the legal practice helps her maintain a piece of her intellectual self.

"Moebius Strip of Work-Life Balance"

Susan B. Myers
Susan Myers' life is like a moebius strip – with more than a couple loops and twists. After Harvard Law School, she set out on her dream to pursue an international law career and make partner. Soon after her son was born, she left big firm practice for an in-house position with a Japanese automobile finance company (somewhat more manageable than being an associate in a law firm). After settling in Japan, her marriage disintegrated. She returned to the U.S., and her life along the path of her moebius strip has led her back to her original law firm.

"My Life-long Commitment to Equal Justice and Civil Rights"

Barbara J. Cox

Barbara Cox decided to become a lawyer at thirteen. She tells her story of alcoholism and drug addition, her desire to protect prisoners in Michigan's state prisons, coming out as a lesbian in college, great success in law school (including law review), teaching legal writing and women's studies at University of Wisconsin, then a tenure-track position at California Western. Her scholarship and service focus on marriage equality and legal rights for same-sex couples.

"New Choices"

Helen I. Zeldes

Helen Zeldes recently joined the work-from-home mommy club. However, cases are flooding in, and big firms want to finance those cases. Prior to law school, Helen worked for herself – starting six businesses (her gallery, number six, is alive and well on Oahu). After being a member of a powerful firm with an army of people to work with, she now answers her own phone, takes conference calls at 6:00 a.m., and spends time with her daughter – going toe-to-toe with the biggest law firms and against the largest corporations in the country.

"Once a Mentor, Always a Mentor"

Samantha S. Goodman

Samantha Goodman has practiced law for almost ten years in a succession of prestigious law firms. She expected to practice in a large firm until she found a more flexible job (one that would allow her to work and raise a family). She married and had two children and has managed to "do it all" – being a working mom and wife – while continuing in large firm practice. It is all possible because of her amazing and supportive mentors (who became her family and dear friends), flexible employers, helpful husband, and a satisfying, fulfilling profession.

"Raising Happy, Productive Children on a Workingwoman's Schedule"

Julie P. Dubick

Julie Dubick has worked for thirty-five years, struggling and succeeding while managing work, family, and marriage. She worked at the U.S. Department of Justice and for the U.S. Marshals Service. She became an associate, then partner at one of San Diego's premier firms – with full time help and a supportive husband. Frustrated by her failure to effect change for women in the firm and just as her two older children were becoming independent, she became pregnant again. She transitioned to stay-at-home mom where she helped found and then head a foundation that makes major gifts to the San Diego community. Now she serves on San Diego Mayor Jerry Sanders' staff.

"Road Less Traveled"

Sara L. May

Sara May didn't know she wanted to be a lawyer. She did know she didn't want to have children. She has stayed true to herself. Early in her legal career, she learned of her love for research and writing and clerked for the courts. She went on to work for a prestigious law firm in San Diego and later returned to become a staff research attorney at the appellate court where she found quality of life. She and her husband decided to return to Denver to family and friends, to an affordable housing market, and to the Colorado Court of Appeals. She and her husband do not have children.

"Tenure at Sixty"

Jacquelyn H. Slotkin

Jackie Slotkin has been a life-long working wife and mother; however, her professional resume is filled with "holes" (reflecting interruptions and readjustments due to marriage and children). Almost twenty years ago, she was hired as a law professor to teach legal research and writing in a non-tenure-track position. She worked hard, became director of the Legal Skills Program, started an LL.M. program for foreign lawyers, produced scholarship, and ultimately received tenure after sixteen years at age sixty.

"You Can Do It All"

Lisa S. Weinreb

Lisa Weinreb's father instilled in her a sense of independence, determination, and pride. She went to college, married, attended law school, had children, became a deputy district attorney (working in the Gang Prosecution Unit), and was elected president of Lawyers Club (the women's bar in San Diego). At times, she questioned whether she could do it all – be a good and involved lawyer, wife, and mother. Her essay explains her "rules" on how to do it all while keeping her sanity.

Introduction

The number of women lawyers has increased dramatically in the past twenty years. Nationally, half of all law students and almost 30% of all lawyers are women. Women lawyers have reached positions of power: women are U.S. Supreme Court justices and state and federal court judges; U.S. Attorneys General and Secretary of State; senators and congresswomen; American Bar Association and American Board of Trial Advocates presidents; university presidents, chief executive officers, and leaders and managing partners of the country's largest law firms. A woman lawyer is running for President of the United States. However, women in the legal profession continue to be underrepresented in positions of greatest status, influence, and economic reward.[1]

Women have increased their presence in all aspects of the profession since 1995: in law firm partnerships, in law schools, as general counsel of major corporations, and in the judiciary.[2] However, women and minority lawyers continue to be underrepresented as partners at major law firms. Even though women account for 50% of the law students and 45% of the associates in law firms, they account for fewer than 16% of all equity

---

[1] See Deborah L. Rhode, ABA COMMISSION ON WOMEN IN THE PROFESSION, THE UNFINISHED AGENDA: WOMEN AND THE LEGAL PROFESSION (2001).
[2] See summary of testimony presented to and data collected by the ABA Commission on Women in the Profession at hearings held in 2003 in ABA COMMISSION ON WOMEN IN THE PROFESSION, CHARTING OUR PROGRESS THE STATUS OF WOMEN IN THE PROFESSION TODAY 2006, at 5.

1

partners.[3] Many women are finding alternatives: working at smaller firms, in-house, for the government, for legal services, and as contract attorneys. In an American Bar Association poll, a third of women expressed the belief that it was not realistic to successfully combine the roles of lawyer, wife, and mother.[4] The number of women lawyers expressing this belief has increased from 13% in 1983 to 33% in 2000.

This book is about women lawyers: women who have struggled to find jobs after law school graduation; women who have experienced conflicts while practicing law (conflicts combining work and family, conflicts with law's confrontations, conflicts due to race, ethnicity, sexual orientation and gender); women who have decided not to practice law; women who have found or chosen alternatives to law practice; women who have found solutions to work-life balance issues; and women who have found practicing law to be the most satisfying profession. The following stories describe those satisfactions and struggles.

I have been a life-long working wife and mother. I have balanced my professional education and career choices with an early marriage, my husband's career, and raising children. I believe I have "done it all" – sequentially (and not all at the same time). I was inspired to create this book because I have been researching female roles since 1976 when I surveyed 200 female college graduates as part of the research for my Ph.D. dissertation. My dissertation explored the decisions each woman had made for herself in her multiple roles, both personally and professionally. In 1996 and in 2002, I expanded my research and surveyed an ethnically diverse population of female lawyers living and working in San Diego to determine if educated women were experiencing role conflict. I am currently completing an article about German women lawyers – an international perspective on women in the legal profession.

---

[3] NAWL NATIONAL SURVEY ON RETENTION AND PROMOTION OF WOMEN IN LAW FIRMS October 2006, at 2.
[4] See Rhode, supra note 1, at 18.

I asked my daughter, Samantha, to be my partner in creating this book since she has been my research and observation laboratory. Sam's life as a law student and lawyer has given me continuing reinforcement for my research about women lawyers. Her career path differed from mine. She attended law school immediately after college, served as an editor on law review, worked as a summer associate, and was offered and accepted a position in a prestigious national law firm after graduation – all before marriage and children. She continues to be an ambitious, dedicated part-time practicing lawyer and loving wife and mother.

Though good lawyering is hard work requiring commitment and responsibility, it can be exciting and fulfilling. Certain themes repeat throughout the essays: the blue suit; women supporting women; inappropriate questions during job interviews and in court; women who have always wanted to be or never wanted to be lawyers; gender discrimination, race discrimination, and discrimination against women with children; the perfect job and the less than perfect work environment; and great and nonexistent mentors.

The book includes essays describing impressive role models and mentors, professional achievement, and remarkable scholarship: the first woman president of ABOTA in fifty years; a deputy district attorney, president of the San Diego women's bar, the Lawyers Club, who offers suggestions for how to "do it all;" women who have published scholarly textbooks and dozens of law review articles; a woman who was former deputy director of the AALS and co-chairs the executive and steering committees of Freedom to Marry; an international crime consultant and founder of the Center for Problem-Oriented Policing; an international human rights advocate; a woman who has started eight successful businesses; and a national CBS legal commentator – stories that inspire and reveal women's progress in the legal profession and in life.

Many of the essays tell unique stories: a street cop who attended Harvard Law School and became a crime consultant and

3

police reformer; a judge whose early life as a private investigator and reporter in Vietnam led her to law school, to private practice, and ultimately to being appointed to the federal bench; an African-American lawyer inspired by family members to become a fourth generation educator; an NLRB attorney whose early struggles helped her relate to her worker-clients; a Mexican-American immigrant who became an immigration lawyer and human rights advocate; an Afro-Cuban Harvard Law School graduate who left her Wall Street firm when her African-American male mentor was denied partnership; a family law attorney, motivated to become a lawyer by her parents' divorce, who started her own firm, had children, then divorced; a lesbian law professor whose scholarship has focused on obtaining and protecting legal recognition for same-sex couples; a mother who left her powerful firm to join the work-from-home mommy club; a woman who followed her dream to pursue a career in intercollegiate athletics after ten years of big firm practice; and many women who have found teaching the most satisfying profession. These stories portray women's advancements in the legal profession while identifying the difficulties, challenges, and barriers.

The women describe balancing personal and professional priorities – some well, others with guilt, all with accommodations including helpful spouses, families, and others: a woman who always knew she did not want children but wanted quality of life which she found as a judicial staff attorney; a big firm partner who juggled family and her profession, then retired to become a full time mother, community volunteer, and consultant on the mayor's staff; a young, single associate at a large national firm who left because the workload allowed no time to even think about life choices such as having children; a large firm attorney, married with children, successfully competing on the part-time track; many women choosing legal education because of its flexible work schedule; a federal government lawyer who juggles marriage, children, and a legal career and attended law school to save her marriage; a sole

4

practitioner and full time mother who plans one day to return to full time practice.

While it may be "harder in heels," the essays are inspiring, observant, introspective, and insightful. Some are humorous, and all are very wise. The women span the age continuum and the range of legal experiences. They are racially and ethnically diverse. Some are married; others are not. Some have children; others have decided not to have children. Though the stories are written by women trained to be lawyers, the stories are applicable to women's lives outside the profession of law and should be lessons for everyone.

Approaching Life as a Lawyer and a Cop

Rana Sampson

Directly after college, a fellowship allowed me to work in New York City government; and as a result, it opened other doors for me. That is how I landed in the Mayor's Office, working on issues related to landmark preservation, the city's ports, and public housing. That was my portfolio. At the time, I planned to apply to law school but decided to put that off because the quality of the work was keeping me engaged.

I was tasked with improving the effectiveness and efficiency of the city agencies in my portfolio. Not surprisingly, I learned a tremendous amount, not the least of which was the power the Mayor's Office held in helping citizens who knew to call with a complaint or a request. The rest of city government moved along as slow as molasses, but direct requests through the Mayor's Office were resolved post haste. How interesting, how easy for those who knew how to short cut their way through delivery of city services. At different points, it occurred to me that anyone could do my job. The power the office brought with it was enough on its own to make things work.

7

While citizens called the office for favors and I helped monitor the efficiency of city services, New York City was undergoing a social upheaval. Crime was rising, eating up neighborhoods. Some landlords in the poorest neighborhoods found it more lucrative to burn down their buildings and collect the fraudulently claimed insurance than it was to maintain the properties. During a World Series game in New York in the late 1970s, the aerial view of Yankee Stadium showed buildings burning nearby as (the late) sports announcer, Howard Cosell, commented, "Ladies and Gentleman, the Bronx is burning." Subways were slathered in graffiti; 42nd Street had become a hangout for pimps and the child prostitutes they exploited, more so than out-of-town theater goers; and the city was sinking fast. Drugs were raging through the city, turning some neighborhoods into "no go" zones, and the vacant lots where arson-snatched buildings once stood became places for open-air drug bazaars. The city was eroding quickly, but not quietly, as its reputation for danger grew with each new, shockingly more violent page one news story.

Where did I fit in? I had always felt grateful for all New York had given me: a free and good public school education; free museums (at that time) and free cultural events; and the stimulating, exciting tapestry of people and neighborhoods. I felt I owed more to the city than working in the most powerful place because working in such a powerful place had too much potential to skew my view of the world and my role in it. Working in the Mayor's Office is something one does at the end of a career, not at the beginning. What would be the opposite – helping people without advantages who are in crisis? After much thought, I decided to become a police officer. I could help people at their most vulnerable and help protect the city at the same time. Clearly a tall order, but where would the young be without idealism?

My colleagues at the Mayor's Office attended my swearing in as a cop; and after six months of academy training, I landed in the northern part of Brooklyn, covering areas that included Bushwick, Williamsburg, and parts of Bedford-Stuyvesant, some of the toughest in the city. I had a foot beat, then a car beat. I delivered babies, made arrests, mediated arguments, helped women beaten by their husbands, and transported the mentally ill through revolving door facilities that emptied them back into neighborhoods only to see some of them pick up a knife again to threaten the imaginary demons that haunted their heads. I volunteered to work as an undercover narcotics officer and was sent to Harlem, Hell's Kitchen (when it was), and the Lower East Side of Manhattan, and saw drug markets and abandoned buildings eat through neighborhoods with the efficiency of acid.

There was always a dual focus: the work on the street and the culture of the department. It was not clear which was more demanding. When I was promoted to sergeant, I felt the sexism in the department even more firmly than I had in my other assignments in the NYPD, and it started on the first day. Sergeants in each precinct changed into uniform in the "sergeants' locker room," not with the patrol officers. It was one of the perks of rank, and it allowed the officers to vent about bosses without them being present. The precinct I was newly assigned to had never had a woman sergeant, thus no women sergeants' locker room. So, when two other women sergeants and I arrived at the precinct (you can just imagine the look of shock on the faces of the officers when they were told they were getting three women sergeants), we were told to use the male sergeants' locker room. It was just as you would imagine in the mid-1980s with porn, stacks of it lying on the room's small table, each magazine more crude and "exotic" than the one before it. Complaining was out of the question; these were our first days as sergeants in an almost exclusively male precinct. It was more important to prove we were equal, not squeamish, with what would be thrown our way. We were hoping to side step the first skirmish but win the war; therefore, we chose to use the same locker room women patrol officers changed in instead, even though it was five flights of stairs above the men's.

Cops, for the most part, are free agents with little supervision and lots of opportunities to do good or not. I had thought I made a reasonable decision to become a cop, but what I saw and experienced left me amazed. All that authority and power, all that discretion, and the reverse of the clientele who called in their requests to the Mayor's Office; the clients in this profession were the abused, the abusers, the poor, the abandoned, the dysfunctional, those warehoused in public housing, the homeless, and of course, the mentally ill. Legal issues, many of them constitutional issues, arose every day (stop and frisk, arrest, and search decisions), and ethical dilemmas punctuated each call for service like a lit fuse. It was almost over the top. It amazed me that more people were not interested in the profession. Only high profile mistakes drew a reproachful crowd. The everyday policing was essentially ignored. For me, I had found my passion. I did not think I could find this mix of problems elsewhere; the crimes, the people, all of it seemed so urgent, and a profession so much in need of new voices and new approaches. As a woman, if I wanted to have an impact on the profession, I felt my voice would be stronger if my credentials were enhanced. I had put off that decision to apply to law school, but now it seemed like the right time.

I attended Harvard. My plan was to return home to New York City and work at the NYPD during the summers. It was an interesting time at the law school: faculty clashes added spice; at the Kennedy School of Government, just a few blocks away, much to my surprise, there were folks convening a few times a year to talk about the future of policing and how much it needed to change. These were later known as Harvard's executive sessions on policing. Things were beginning to move in policing. Perhaps the field was opening up. There was a push to open dialogue with the community, a push to understand that police legitimacy requires a connectedness to both the community and the law. And that trust is much more easily built when the police agree to be guided by the constitution rather than to circumvent it.

While at law school that first year, I wrote to the Police Commissioner thanking him for granting my leave of absence to attend the first year of law school and said I was willing to work on any assignment the department needed during the summer (and hoped for a second leave of absence in September so I could attend my second year). I did not hear back, so I returned as a sergeant to my patrol assignment in my former precinct once summer began. It seemed like less than two seconds had passed before I was told to report to headquarters pronto. I was to meet with a high ranking official in NYPD's personnel office. When I did, he said to me that the chief of personnel's secretary was going on leave for the summer, and they would like me to replace her. I sat there stunned. "They" would never have asked a male sergeant to be a secretary. After discarding all the things I really wanted to say, disrespecting rank would not have been tolerated, I settled on the lie, "I'm sorry sir, I don't type." He said, "You mean to tell me that you go to Harvard Law School and you don't type?" Well now, that's quite interesting; it meant I was being punished, perhaps not by everyone in the upper ranks but certainly by this man. For what? For attending a good law school? Apparently, I did not know my place. At the time, there were 24,000 cops in the NYPD. Many were very good but the ones who weren't could certainly give you heartburn. I ended the conversation by saying, "I'm sorry sir, that's not the focus of the curriculum."

Fast forward; after all, this is just a short story. I am a lawyer, but my work is as a crime consultant and police reformer. Sometimes the story of how you get to the place is just as important as the place you ultimately end up. Through that journey, I worked at a national police think tank, at the White House on crime policy as a White House Fellow, at a university as head of public safety, and as a crime reduction and policing reform consultant. I have authored publications about crime and about more advanced approaches to crime reduction. I have consulted across the United States and internationally on these issues. Along with several colleagues, we founded the Center for Problem-Oriented Policing, where researched approaches for effective policing are available free for citizens and for police alike. The U.S. Department of Justice has provided financial support for our Center.

Much is left to be done. Sometimes in policing, it's two steps forward and one step back (we all know the high profile incidents that make us reel). But two steps for one is still a gain, still a change, still an improvement from where it was, although it seems more so for some police agencies than others. There remains unevenness in policing; some agencies confuse over aggressiveness and zero tolerance with effective policing, when proactive policing can be done equitably and smartly, widening the tools cops use rather than narrowing them to their gun belt. My law degree helped me, no doubt. It gave me access to the profession in a different way; it fine tuned my thinking. I always approach my work as a lawyer, actually, as a lawyer and a cop.

B.A., Barnard College, Columbia University, J.D., Harvard Law School. Rana Sampson is a national crime consultant and the former director of public safety for the University of San Diego. She was previously a White House Fellow; National Institute of Justice Fellow; senior researcher and trainer at the Police Executive Research Forum; attorney; and patrol officer, undercover narcotics officer, and patrol sergeant with the New York City Police Department, where she was awarded several commendations of merit and won the National Improvement of Justice Award. She is the author of numerous publications about crime and safety on a variety of topics: drug dealing in privately owned apartment complexes, bullying in schools, acquaintance rape of college students, domestic violence, false burglar alarms, and misuse and abuse of 911. She is the coauthor (with Michael Scott) of Tackling Crime and Other Public-Safety Problems: Case Studies in Problem-Solving, which documents high-quality crime control efforts from around the United States, Canada, and Europe. Rana is a founding member of the Center for Problem-Oriented Policing. She is a judge for the Herman Goldstein Award for Excellence in Problem-Oriented Policing, a former judge for the police Fulbright awards, and a former commissioner with California's Commission on Peace Officer

Standards and Training. She is married to San Diego Mayor Jerry Sanders.

Becoming a Lawyer: An Immigrant's Challenge

Lilia S. Velasquez

Law school is a challenge for anyone; but as an immigrant from Mexico, the challenge seemed more like a pipe dream. At the age of nineteen, my family decided to move to the United States. With some reluctance and limited knowledge of the English language, I decided to join them. I could not attend high school because I was older than eighteen. Wanting to pursue higher education, I attended two junior colleges where I struggled to learn English. Despite the language and cultural difficulties, I graduated from San Diego State University with a Bachelor's Degree in Social Work. It was after completing my baccalaureate degree that I decided to apply to law school. My GPA from college was very good, but my score on the Law School Admission Test (LSAT) was marginal. California Western School of Law accepted me under its diversity program.

Law School, the Bar Exam, and My Family

At the time I entered law school in 1978, I was already married and had a two-year-old daughter, Sandra. Being married and having a child had not deterred me from pursuing my dream of attending law school. Though I was terrified because of my English language limitations, I welcomed the challenge with enthusiasm. It was fortunate that close to the law school was a day-care program my daughter could attend while I was in school. Law school proved to be as hard as I had imagined. Of an entering class of 325, there were four Hispanic students, two or three African-Americans, and a few Asian students. It was intimidating to be in a classroom with more than 150 students and to be the only Hispanic student. I felt I stood out like a sore thumb, and I was terrified I would be called on to speak in class.

I found I had to study harder than most because of my language deficiency. My first disappointment came when I received the grade for my first law school exam in criminal law. I received a C-, and I was devastated. When I was a student in Mexico, I was one of the top students in my class, and it was hard to be confronted with a mediocre grade. Once I recovered from the shock, I went to see my professor, hoping to learn he had made a mistake, or at least, why I had done so poorly. The professor reviewed my exam and pointed out the issues I left out and how I should have structured, analyzed, and written the exam. It was a lesson in humility and a warning that if I did not improve my writing skills, I could be terminated from school.

Rather than dwell on my first law school failure, I decided to study harder and to change my approach to writing exams. The following semester, I received an A in criminal procedure; with this small success – and a huge boost in self-confidence – I realized I was capable of graduating from law school. It also taught me that when in trouble, there is no shame in seeking help. I managed to graduate in two and one half years, rather than the normal three years.

16

During my last semester of law school, my second daughter, Elena, was born. She was not planned, and the pregnancy made my last semester very stressful. My infant daughter's birth also meant I had to care for her while I studied for the bar exam. By then, my English had improved significantly; but my comprehension was slower than the rest of my classmates. As a result, I had to study harder and continuously during that last semester and during preparation for the bar exam.

Having two daughters to care for plus studying every day for the bar exam was an experience I will never forget. I never gave up. The way I saw it, the bar exam was just another exam. The most important thing in my life was my family, my husband, and my two daughters. I reasoned that if I did not pass the bar exam, I would still have them; and my life would not be over. When I took the bar exam, pass rates were less than 50%. This increased my determination to pass the bar. It was a challenge, and I willingly met it.

When I took the bar exam, my daughter Elena was eight months old; and I was still nursing. My husband would bring our daughter during the lunch break, and we would go to Balboa Park. I would nurse my daughter and then eat lunch before returning to take the afternoon part of the exam. Many of my school friends told me I had the perfect excuse to fail the bar, given my background and two young daughters. But fortunately, I passed the bar exam on the first try. Two of my Hispanic classmates did not pass, and their disappointment saddened me.

Minority students, foreign students, or immigrant students like me struggle more than others in law school. For me, the challenge was the language barrier. For other students, years of educational deficiencies followed them to law school. For many others, the obstacle to success was their lack of self-esteem. Because of my struggles in law school, I am concerned with the attrition rate of minority students in law school.

Law Career Choices

My background as an immigrant also helped me to choose the area of law I wanted to practice. As a law student, I gained experience helping immigrants through the civil law clinic at the law school; and I also served as an intern for a nonprofit organization that assisted indigent immigrants. Because of my background, I had an affinity for working with immigrants. Also, it helped that I was fluent in Spanish and received the highest grade in immigration law. With great excitement, I opened my own office in the Chamber Building in October 1985.

I have practiced immigration law exclusively for the past twenty-one years; in 1991, I became a certified immigration law specialist. I have built a thriving practice with two associates, law school interns, and clerical staff. Becoming an immigration lawyer was the right decision for me. I not only like what I do, but I am truly passionate about my work.

I was invited to become an adjunct law professor. I often see minority and immigrant students suffer with poor grades. If their performance falls below a certain average, they may be terminated from law school after their first year. Some students have told me they can improve their analytical skills or overcome their writing deficiencies by studying harder. Others struggle with marginal grades, graduate, and never pass the bar exam. This issue is important to me, because it hurts when a minority student in my class is terminated for poor grades. I feel these students could have been saved and would have been able to continue with school had they sought help from their professors. As an immigrant and a minority attorney, I feel responsible for helping them. I have joined mentorship programs with various associations and have also volunteered as a mentor to my own students who need that extra attention.

My Clients

Advocating for the rights of immigrants and refugees is frustrating at times, but it is also rewarding. Our system of justice is

18

not perfect, and immigrants and refugees are often denied access to justice because they lack adequate representation or they simply do not know how to access the court system. Too frequently, moreover, immigrants are the victims of fraud by unscrupulous immigration consultants and even by unethical lawyers.

My background, language skills, and cultural sensitivity have given me an opportunity to help those immigrants, refugees, and asylees who are most vulnerable: people whose civil rights have been violated, refugee women who have fled gender persecution, victims who have been trafficked, and women victims of domestic violence. When I hear women's stories of personal hardship and survival, I am inspired and motivated. It makes me realize how lucky I am to have the knowledge and ability to help them navigate the legal system and to be able to make a difference in their lives. It is touching to receive their gratitude and small tokens of appreciation, especially when they thought their cases were impossible to win.

Local Community Contributions

As lawyers, we cannot confine our energies to individual representation; we also need to become active politically, lobby to effect needed changes in the law, and educate audiences everywhere about their rights. As an expert in the field of immigration law, I participate as often as I can. On a weekly television show, for example, I provide legal advice to our viewers on relevant immigration issues. I also participate in seminars throughout San Diego County, counseling indigent immigrants about their rights and speaking out as an activist on the current immigration debate.

While the U.S. Congress continues to struggle to find an answer to the more than eleven million undocumented migrants, we in San Diego have seen an increase in hate crimes, approval of day labor ordinances that prevent day laborers from getting jobs, and even a city council ordinance denying housing to undocumented migrants. As things have become more difficult for immigrants and refugees, we need more than ever committed immigration advocates to defend the rights of the vulnerable in our society.

Immigration law is one of those categories of great importance in the 21st century. The world is smaller because of technology, and globalization makes it easier for people to migrate to different parts of the world. Increased immigration into the United States has also created discrimination, "compassion fatigue" for refugees, and groups of individuals who have taken the law into their own hands by attempting to arrest undocumented migrants. The events of 9/11 have also generated anti-immigrant hysteria, and many see immigrants as potential terrorists. As a result of the current anti-immigrant climate, immigrants have suffered a backlash, and it has become more frustrating to represent immigrants and refugees before the Department of Homeland Security bureaucracy.

Global, International Contributions

My work as a human rights advocate for women has taken me to many parts of the world. I have presented at the U.N.'s *Fourth World Conference on Women* in Beijing, at the U.N.'s Human Rights Commission in Geneva, and at various international forums. In Nepal, I worked with women's groups on the issues of human trafficking for commercial sexual exploitation, the denial of citizenship to children born out of wedlock, and the rights of the *Dalit* women, among others. My background and experience as a woman lawyer have enabled me to train and empower women in other parts of the world, training them how to draft and propose legislation in their home countries, how to create and present public service announcements in the media, and how to educate other women about their rights.

I have also been privileged to work with lawyers and judges in Latin America, providing training in trial skills, cross-cultural negotiation, and media advocacy. Being an immigrant and being fluent in Spanish are assets that have opened doors for me in many countries. As an adjunct professor of immigration law, foreign students look to me as a role model, a professional who provides proof that if I could do it, they can do it, too. My experience of having attended law school when there were few minority students has helped me encourage others who are similarly situated.

Recognition

As a result of my dedication in assisting immigrants, I have been given numerous awards: the *Othli* Award, the highest recognition given by the government of Mexico to individuals who assist immigrants, and the *Fay Stender* Award, given in 2005 by the California Women's Lawyers Association. The latter award was in recognition of my efforts in advancing the ideal of equal justice for all, particularly immigrant women who have been oppressed and victimized. Being recognized by my peers is very important to me. But what provides me with the greatest satisfaction is winning a tough case, and my clients' emotional hugs for having saved them from being sent to a country where they may be killed or seriously harmed. I believe most women enter the legal profession to make a difference in society. In my field of work, obtaining asylum for a woman who was persecuted because of her gender or obtaining a visa for a child who was a victim of human trafficking for sexual exploitation are the best rewards.

Balance

Like most women lawyers, I have struggled to balance my work as a lawyer with family responsibilities. I am sure I am not alone in feeling guilty for not spending enough time with my children, for not staying home to care for them, for not attending all the PTA meetings, and for not baking them cookies on a regular basis. Thanks to the support of my husband, Luis, I managed to raise two beautiful and intelligent daughters who have succeeded academically and are strong feminists. No matter how I rationalize the benefits of working while my two daughters were young, the fact remains I sacrificed spending more time with them for the sake of practicing my profession. Coming from a conservative, Latin background, the decision was more difficult for me. I still remember one day when my five-year-old daughter asked me, "Who is more important, us or your illegal alien clients?" Although she made me laugh, I also knew there was truth in her honest questions.

Achieving success as a lawyer is not something extraordinary just because I am an immigrant. I believe many of us face hardships because of our backgrounds. But whatever struggles we face, they can be overcome if we work hard, believe in ourselves, and have the support of family and friends. I hope that through my work and example, I can serve as an inspiration to other immigrant women to pursue their dreams of becoming lawyers.

J.D., California Western School of Law, LL.M., University of San Diego. Lilia Velasquez is an internationally recognized human rights advocate in immigration law. Most recently, she has successfully represented victims of trafficking for prostitution and obtained legal status for them in the U.S. She is an adjunct professor at California Western School of Law and an instructor in Oral Advocacy and Indigenous Project Director with Proyecto ACCESO. Red is Lilia's signature clothing color, her nickname is "La Flama" for the flame of justice, and her license plate reads Flama.

Canary in Coal Mine

Whittney Graham-Beard

In my second year of law school, I participated in the school's "On-Campus Interview Program" to get a job with one of the many law firms that participated in the program. I was a great candidate – I was at the top of my class; I had worked for a large, New York-based law firm during the summer between my 1L and 2L years; and I had an outgoing personality. To top it all off, in the fall of 1998, the economy was on fire and law firms were practically throwing jobs at anyone with a pulse. For me, the interview process was not about whether I would get a good summer job, but which one I would choose.

It was with this feeling of confidence that I entered one of many short, on-campus interviews. This particular interview was with a smaller, San Diego-based firm. They had sent one representative to conduct their interviews, a man in his mid-forties. I sat across the table from him wearing a conservative, navy blue skirt suit. I wore a skirt suit because the ladies of my class had been advised by career services that wearing a pants suit to an interview, a mere fourteen months before the *year 2000*, could be viewed by some interviewers as flippant. A woman deigning to wear pants might reveal herself to be someone who likes to flout convention a little too much. Never mind that we were applying to become the next generation of zealous advocates. We knew enough to avoid being seen as too willing to push boundaries.

The interviewer and I sat and chatted for awhile as he asked the requisite questions – why had I chosen to attend law school, how did I enjoy my previous summer experience, did I really compete in "tournament bowling" as the interests section of my resume had indicated? After he was done with his questions, he asked if I had any for him. In fact, I did. In researching his firm, I had noted that the firm had very few female lawyers among their ranks. Not only were they lacking female partners, a fact that was not terribly out of the ordinary, they only had a few female associates as well. Given the ratio of men to women in law school by the late 1990s, I asked what could explain the lack of young women lawyers at his firm? He let out a sigh and cocked his head to one side as he leaned forward to give me his surprisingly candid and patronizing response. "Well, Whittney," he began, "let me just start by saying, being a lawyer is hard. It can be a difficult lifestyle, and it's just plain hard work." I sat there looking at him, wondering what he could possibly be getting at. Did he think I had gotten this far in my legal education without realizing that lawyers work hard? And, what does that have to do with female attorneys anyway? He was about to let me know. He continued, "Look at it from my perspective. If I have a male candidate and a female candidate with roughly the same credentials, I have a tough hiring decision to make. It takes a lot of time and energy to train an associate. After working for a few years, you may want to start a family; and the lifestyle of a lawyer at a big firm is probably not going to suit you anymore. Men are less likely to leave to raise a family." I sat across from him, eyes wide with disbelief, mulling over what he had said. My mind raced with questions. If his answer were a law school hypothetical posed by a professor, how many state and federal laws did he just violate? Why did he assume I wanted a family? I'm not even married. Am I going to fail at being a lawyer because I can't hack it with a family? I can't believe he just said all that!

24

With that, he summed up his answer by saying that was why his firm had more male than female associates and asked if I had any more questions. Despite the fact that I had at least five more minutes of time left for my interview, I abruptly said no. I had learned everything I needed to know about his firm and cut the interview short. Later, when I relayed the story to my friends at the law school, many of them, both male and female, suggested I make a formal complaint with the career services office. The firm would be banned from our school for such a blatant and sexist violation of law and school policy. But for some odd reason, I was not as upset about it after the fact as I thought I would be. Maybe I had misunderstood, or he had made his point very badly. Perhaps he was just saying they have few women because all the women they have hired have left to start families – not that they preemptively avoided hiring women because of that possibility. Any way I looked at it, I decided it was not important. He had shown himself to be either sexist or an ineffective communicator, or both. I wanted nothing to do with a firm that would choose him as its representative. There was no need to report my experience. I would just forget about it and move on to bigger and better things.

Several years later, I was working as an attorney at a large law firm. Oddly enough, the majority of the associates I worked with were women. Contrary to the prediction made by the gentleman during that interview, we were not fleeing the firm to start families in droves. We were staying and working hard. We were enjoying our financial freedom and professional success. We were equals with our male counterparts. Unlike the women dreamed up by my sexist interviewer, we were not running from the firm to start families. Unlike generations of women before us, we were staying in high-stress, high salary jobs longer and longer. We were each getting closer to the brass ring of partnership. However, the reason was not some startling new form of feminism or new type of woman. For the most part, we were not leaving the firm to start families because there were no families to start. No men on bended knee, pleading to be ours forever. We were working like our male counterparts; but unlike them, there was no huge pool of the opposite sex waiting to date women like us. Of course, there were exceptions; but it was true for many of us that our hours and workload were not conducive to finding and growing lasting romance.

Then one day, a friend of mine brought in the latest *Time* magazine. On the cover was a picture of an adorable, chubby baby sitting on top of a pile of papers. The cover shouted "Babies vs. Career: Which Should Come First for Women Who Want Both?" And then quietly under that text was the line that changed the mood of every woman in my department: "The harsh facts about FERTILITY." Every woman I worked with at the time was unmarried, and most of us did not even have the time to date seriously. We were all around thirty. Inside the pages of that magazine, we were told that our eggs had begun deteriorating at an alarming rate from the time we turned twenty-seven. We learned that our chances of having a normal, healthy baby, or even conceiving, diminished with every week we got closer to forty. The news was not good. At least, not for us. The level of stress about this article was palpable throughout our office for the next few days.

About a week later, most of us had forgotten about the *Time* article, or at least put it out of our minds. Every so often, usually around midnight after a string of long nights, the conversation among my female co-workers would turn to our love lives and whether we would ever find a meaningful relationship while we worked as though we were men (who didn't have to concern themselves with aging ovaries or finding a mate with fantastic earning potential). It was an uncomfortable thought. We were smart, strong, hard-working, and had earned our success. But for most us who did want families, the reality of the situation was bleak. We had few female role models to pattern ourselves after. Women partners with families were few and far between, and even they seemed like superwomen who survived on three hours of sleep per night while handing their children off to nannies or stay-at-home dads.

26

Nonetheless, we continued working at the firm despite our concerns. Ultimately, I left big firm life for many reasons. I was unhappy with my workload and my lifestyle – not because there were little ones toddling to the door to greet me at night. I was unhappy because my social and family life seemed to be shrinking while my work life consumed more and more of my attention. At some point, for me anyway, the freedom and luxury the job provided no longer outweighed the sacrifices I was making. Those sacrifices included the possibility of having a family. They also included many other joys foregone, like being an active member of my community and spending time with my parents. Many of my female colleagues are still in firms. Some have left.

Sometimes I wonder if that interviewer was right to mistrust me and my willingness to go the long haul. He saw me as a woman who would not go the distance for black and white reasons. In a way, he was right because much of my concern about the lifestyle of a lawyer was centered around the realities of being a woman who wants to procreate someday. But, in many ways, he was wrong. I left the large law firm because I wanted to have a life outside of my career. Too often, what is expected of lawyers is that they give up much of their lives outside the office. Women, because we often take on the task of child rearing and have physical limits on our fertility, reject this lifestyle sooner and more often than men. Perhaps, instead of mistrusting female candidates for their propensity to care more about their personal lives than the office, law firms would do better to consider there is another way to practice law. Just because men don't leave at the rate women do does not mean they are not making equally serious and sometimes tragic sacrifices in their personal lives. Maybe instead of dismissing female flight from the profession as an idiosyncrasy of the fairer sex, the legal field should consider our exodus as a warning that law should not be practiced in such an increasingly high-pressured way. Indeed, many partners I worked for expressed that in their long experience in the profession, the pressure to bill more and more hours had begun to build to levels they had never imagined when the began practicing. Maybe the problem is not women entering a profession in which they cannot hack it. Perhaps, instead, women are like the canary in the coal mine, warning the profession that it must become more humane if all lawyers are to remain happy and satisfied while practicing law.

B.A., magna cum laude, University of California at San Diego, J.D., University of California, Los Angeles School of Law, Order of the Coif. She served as a managing editor for the UCLA Women's Law Journal and was a teaching assistant for Lawyering Skills and Torts. She clerked for the Honorable Jerry Buchmeyer, then Chief Judge of the U.S. District Court for the Northern District of Texas in Dallas. She practiced in the Los Angeles office of Milbank, Tweed, Hadley & McCloy LLP, in the global corporate department, and coordinated the firm's participation in the Public Counsel Adoptions Project. She is a Teaching Fellow at California Western School of Law.

Everything I Needed to Know for Life I Learned in First Grade

The Honorable Louisa S. Porter

<u>My Early Years</u>

In the 1950s, schools in the United States, including Fort Wayne, Indiana, where I grew up, were fond of Achievement Tests. These tests were given to children in their early years of elementary school; and, from the results, teachers would determine a child's future learning abilities and potential life achievement. These tests were the death knell for shy students like me. Yes me! No one who knows me now would ever believe I was once shy. But shy I was. I did not talk until I was three! When I finally decided to talk, however, it was in full sentences. My uncle joked he had never seen me until I was seven. I was so shy I hid under the dining room table whenever a stranger approached our door. My uncle was hardly a stranger, but my reaction to him describes the depth of my shyness. I came out from under the table about the same time the results of the Achievement Test advised my mother (and me) that I would never be more than a C student. It was apparent the only person who was going to prove them wrong was me. To this day, if anyone says "you cannot do that," "that" is exactly what I do.

I somehow propelled myself from interminable shyness to leader of the pack. In retrospect, I find it difficult to imagine how I got from where I began to where I am today. I attribute it to my divine God and the lessons I learned along the way.

Growing up, I had no concept of, and refused to recognize any difference between, black, white, or purple. For example, when I had a slumber party for my tenth birthday, I insisted on inviting all the girls in my class, including Dorothy, the sole Black member of the class. Needless to say, in Indiana in the 1950s, Dorothy and I were the only two attending my birthday slumber party. However, in life's lessons, I was the winner – it was a great party.

When I graduated from college, which was a major accomplishment in itself since I was the first in my family to do so, I moved to Indianapolis. I had not earned my "Mrs." degree, the goal of many young women in the 1960s. Nor was I interested in shopping for a husband at that time in my life. I was too young with too many places to go and people to see. However, as a female in 1969, fresh from Indiana University with my bachelor's degree, the only jobs available were clerical or government. I chose government, a social security disability adjudicator and vocational specialist for the State of Indiana, earning less than $400 per month.

I also had no credit, and credit card offers were not rushing in with every mail delivery. This was certainly not happening for women in the 1960s; women gained credibility and financial status through their husbands. I knew that to survive, I absolutely had to establish credit. Since my sister was a sales girl (which is what sales associates were called in 1969) at a local department store, I applied for a credit card there. My sister hand delivered my application. I thought it was odd when a senior vice president contacted me to discuss my application and even more so when he insisted on setting an appointment to discuss the matter after regular business hours. At the appointment he asked, "Do you party?" I naively

30

responded, "I love parties." He approved my credit card on the spot. Three days later my card arrived, and three weeks later the calls arrived – calls from visiting businessmen in need of companionship for the night. I changed my telephone number and learned another invaluable life lesson: I would never again allow myself to be placed in such a compromising position. It was my job, and mine alone, to make sure it never happened again.

I attended university during the Vietnam War and the draft. I was an activist and very outspoken in my criticism of the discriminatory draft that excluded women. I was not so bold as to join the military, but I made my position well known. Shortly after graduation and while working at my government job, I received a call from an unknown source. "So, you want to go to Vietnam, huh?" My response was, "Yes." "Do you have a passport?" And I answered, "Yes." The following Tuesday, I was on a jet heading half way around the world to Vietnam. I was issued Vietnamese and U.S. press credentials to travel and to cover the October 1971 Presidential election. I traveled by every known form of transport including dugout boat through the Mekong Delta at a time when it was enemy held and controlled. I observed, interviewed, and wrote. Why did I go? Because someone said, "Women cannot go to Vietnam."

Since I was already halfway around the world, I took advantage of an offer from TWA – for $100 more, I could circle the world and make as many stops as I wanted. I visited Taipei, Japan, Hong Kong, Cambodia, Thailand, India, Israel, Egypt, Paris, Belgium, and even London before I came home. When I returned to Indianapolis, I started my own private investigation business. It was just me – no employees. I literally sold myself by going door to door (cold calls) to law firms and insurance companies. Soon, based solely on my street moxy, I had eleven paying clients. However, I had no car and no telephone. I used the telephone booth one and a half blocks from my apartment and either borrowed a car, taxied, or walked to my job assignments. Things were fine until the winter of 1973 when Indianapolis experienced the worst storms in history.

With snow piled up to my knees and with more expected, the walk to the telephone booth was no longer a viable alternative. I bought a car and had telephone service installed. My business flourished.

But that was not enough for me. I watched my attorney clients (eight law firms) and realized I was doing all the work, and I was just as bright and analytical as they were. They, however, were making $40 an hour compared to my $7 an hour. It was at that point I decided to attend law school.

Law School and Legal Career

I applied anywhere I would not suffer from hay fever. The University of San Diego School of Law was the first to respond with an offer. In the summer of 1974, I loaded up my TR6 sports car with my clothes and my pillow, on which I placed my dear puppy, Taipei Porter, and drove across the country to my new home. I fell in love with San Diego the minute I arrived and swore I would rather sell pencils on a street corner than return to Indiana.

In 1977, I graduated from the USD Law School with honors and started the arduous task of finding my first law-related job. Because I had worked for insurance companies in Indiana, no plaintiff's firm would hire me. Because I had worked as a private investigator for a plaintiff's firm while in law school, no defense firm would hire me. When all I had left was $400, just enough for my last month's rent, I found a job with a two-man plaintiff's personal injury firm. At that time, my salary was $15,000 per year. I was there less than three months when the two partners split the firm. I stayed with one of the partners long enough to establish myself with the local bar, then started my own practice. I established my clientele the same way I had started the PI business: I met with attorneys whose practices did not include personal injury and sold them on the idea of referring those cases to me. I assured them I would not steal their clients. In San Diego in the late 1970s, there were only a handful of female trial attorneys. I became one of them. I loved juries and juries loved me. The practice was good to me, and my clients were well-served.

My organizational and leadership skills were put to rapid use. I became an active member of the then-San Diego Trial Lawyers Association (SDTLA) and the San Diego County Bar Association (SDCBA). I worked my way up the leadership core of both organizations. I served as president of SDTLA in 1988 and secretary of SDCBA in 1991. Both organizations prepared me to chair the bench/bar committee, the liaison between the bench and the county bar association. From this position, I became interested and involved in the administrative functioning of the courts. I liked being part of the solution.

Living My Dream: New Challenges

None of this was enough. I am a dreamer. My whole life I have loved to day dream, always thinking about how to attain those dreams. My life-long dream was to have the ultimate freedom: to fly like a bird, to lift myself above the commotion of life, to look down on the world while transporting myself to another place. But, "Girls do not fly!" So, I traded my legal skills for flight lessons; and ultimately, I accomplished my dream of obtaining my private pilot's license. Today, I am the proud owner of my own flying machine, a four-seat, single engine Piper dubbed "Ms. America." Ms. America is truly my own; she has nose art I designed – a picture of me flying the American flag.

In 1990, after almost fifteen years practicing law, I attended an air/space show at Brown Field in San Diego. The show included air demonstrations and educational lectures. The lawyer for the Smithsonian Air and Space Museum in Washington, D.C., introduced me to Space Law, a concept that, at that time, was beyond my earth-bound imagination. He talked of the precursor to a constitution for outer space travelers and residents, the Declaration of First Principles in Space. I was hooked, smitten, and the dream machine went into full gear. I applied to McGill University Law School in Montreal, Canada, and was accepted to the LL.M. program in Space Law. McGill was one of the few – and the closest – law schools in the world to offer a space law curriculum. My husband of only five years and I purchased boots for the harsh Canadian winters (for us and for our dogs). We started the process of renting our home and figuring out what to do with both of our law practices during our two years in Montreal.

During the same time period in early December 1990, I attended the annual SDCBA reception when I was approached by no less than five lawyers and judges, all of whom urged me to apply for the position of Magistrate Judge with the U.S. District Court, Southern District of California. Each claimed the job and I were made for one another.

A new challenge! I applied. Before I knew it, I was in the final five of eighty-nine applicants and scheduled for final interviews with the judges of the court. Decision time was fast approaching. What if they offered me the job? What about those boots we had purchased for the Montreal winters? What of my dreams of space law? I soon realized I was about to reach yet another cross-road in my life. I knew that whichever road I took, it would be the right one for me. I had received so much support from my husband, friends, and acquaintances in the bar that, although I was still undecided, when the call came from Chief Judge Judith Keep offering the position, I said yes.

Marriage and Family

Although I have never had the "maternal instinct," I certainly have a need to care for and nurture. In 1971, a college friend called to tell me his dog was having puppies, and he wanted me to have one. I initially declined because I felt my working life was too busy for a puppy. Yet, shortly before Valentine's Day 1972, I found myself in my car, driving from Indianapolis to Gary in a heavy winter snow storm, to pick up Taipei Porter (named for the capital of China where I had recently visited). On my way back to Indianapolis, Taipei Porter threw up all over my new car. From that point on, I knew she needed nurturing, and my love affair with dogs began.

Despite the fullness my pups have brought to my life (there have been six pups over the last four decades), at age thirty-seven, I

34

suffered the biological time clock syndrome familiar to many professional women. Had I missed a major experience in life? Who would care about me when I became old? Have I wasted a perfectly good life for work? All good questions. At the time, my law practice was doing well. As a solo practitioner, I could not afford to take time away to have a child because the practice would have crumbled. It seemed to me there was no way I could do it all.

Nevertheless, I had the good fortune, at the age of thirty-nine, to fall in love and marry. My husband, who was forty-seven at the time with a family from a prior marriage, added joy to my life in many ways. With a new husband and a new family, there were so many things to do, places to go, and special times to enjoy. At the time, a child did not fit into our lives. I am not sorry for my decision not to have children.

In addition to my life on the bench (sixteen years now), my job as a judge has afforded me the opportunity to meet and to work with many bright, young minds. As a judge, I have had the great fortune to hire law clerks to assist me with my judicial duties. I have mentored and nurtured each of my law clerks, and all have gone on to become fabulous lawyers and people. My law clerks have become part of my huge extended family, and I will never be lonely. My life is so blessed with husband, friends, family, professional satisfaction, and beautiful puppies – all have made my life complete.

B.A., Indiana University, J.D., with honors, University of San Diego. Judge Porter is a federal magistrate judge, U.S. District Court, Southern District of California. She was a private investigator before law school, then a civil litigator in private practice before being appointed to the federal bench in 1991, where she was the presiding judge from 1997-2002. She is a Master of the Bench, Louis Welsh Inn of Court. She is a frequent lecturer on legal issues, domestic and international, and the author of articles on international legal issues.

Her many passions include flying her Piper aircraft, Ms. America, and a four-decade love affair with dogs.

Evolution of Choice

Donna Marie D'Angelo Melby

January 17, 2005, was more than a special occasion. As I prepared to slip into the most beautiful evening gown I have ever had occasion to own, I thought about what I might say in two hours when I would have the professional privilege of a lifetime – being formally installed as national President of the American Board of Trial Advocates (ABOTA). This was truly the honor of my professional life. In the almost fifty year history of this esteemed organization that dedicates itself to the preservation of the Seventh Amendment right to civil trial by jury and includes among its members many of the most accomplished plaintiff and defense civil jury trial lawyers in the country, no woman had ever been elected to serve as president.

As I prepared for the black tie event, I looked around the hotel room at the flowers my dear women, professional friends had sent from all over the country. I was overcome by emotion as thoughts of the last thirty years flashed across the screen of my mind. I marveled at the evolution of a career that seemed to begin not so long ago, at how fortunate I felt, and how I never imagined so much good fortune would become mine through pursuit of my dream to become the best jury trial lawyer I could be.

Thoughts of my parents, now deceased, my family, and my dear friends, most of them lawyers who had traveled great distances from across the country to be here, occupied my mind. I paused, silently, to give thanks for the many gifts our noble profession has bestowed upon me. At the same time I thought about the often uphill struggle through the sometimes rocky professional terrain that was an undeniable and an integral part of the last thirty years. At the same moment, I was instantly content in the knowledge that, for many more reasons than I could possibly express, the journey, though admittedly harder than it should have been, had been worth it.

I transitioned to thoughts of an article I had read recently. A young woman lawyer, while being interviewed by a prominent legal publication, expressed her view that the generation of women who had preceded her must not have been very "smart." With an obvious lack of personal knowledge, she declared, "These women sacrificed too much." For reasons unclear to her, this same young woman noted, with apparent disdain, that the women in previous generations had tolerated too much: they allowed what she apparently would not have allowed, and they were silent when she would not have been.

The interview painted a harsh reality. At least some, and potentially many professional women younger than me, do not know or perhaps, even worse, do not care that the professional options available today would literally not exist but for the women she had so seriously maligned. Indeed, in less than thirty years, things have changed. She seemed oblivious to the fact that no one would be interviewing her – about what career path to choose or comparing leave policies of one firm to another – without the sacrifice of women, including me, who had preceded her in the profession. These important facts were entirely lost on her.

With some recognition of the fact that the path to success as a woman litigator is fraught with gender specific hurdles, work-life "balance" continues to be the focus of nearly every article about and interview with "successful" women lawyers. When I began practicing law almost thirty years ago, such things were not on the radar screen of most private law firms. When I applied for my first job, the firms I interviewed with had no women lawyers. Navigation of the legal terrain between then and now was mostly one of "firsts" and "only."

The multiple interview questions I was asked are all illegal now. Diversity objectives did not exist then; neither did maternity leave policies. Mention of either would brand a female job applicant immediately as a "radical" and insure she would not be hired. The goal was to get a job as a lawyer and then to keep it, with the hope that you would not be asked too many times to get the coffee, and that maybe some kind male colleague might think to include you in a lunch or client event. I soon learned these were unrealistic expectations. By way of example, I recall sitting at my desk at around four in the afternoon when I noticed that all the lawyers, except for me (and including the ones hired from my law school class), had left the office. Of course, I was the only woman lawyer in the firm. The next day I discovered all of them had attended a client event at an all male club where the entertainers wore no clothes. The clients were men and the lawyers were men; there was no place for someone like me. The role models, for me, were quite simply, nonexistent.

There is no way to sugar coat the path to partnership as a female litigation partner in an international law firm. Balance has mostly been absent. By the time my son was five years old, he knew what it meant for his mother to be in trial. A palpable feeling in my stomach returns immediately whenever I vividly recall his question: "Mom, when will this trial be over?" He knew what it meant for his life when trial was in session and when it was not.

But the truth is that while we can never pretend it has been easy, the years of hard work and sacrifice have been worthwhile. The gifts of a profession for which I have always had a passion have been many. Many of my very best friends are my professional colleagues, including some who became clients and some I have had the privilege of partnering with for many years.

I am the eldest of five daughters. My mother married at eighteen years of age, never worked outside the home, and gave birth to me when she was just nineteen years old. My father was ten years my mother's senior. His early and untimely death at age forty-nine, when I was a second year college student, was no less than total devastation to me. My youngest sister was only nine years old at the time and my mom just thirty-nine. She fell apart completely. So did I. I came very close to dropping out of college. There was not enough money, and my mother and sisters needed me. I could not seem to pull myself out of the depths of darkness and despair.

I recall my mother saying to me that my father would never have wanted me to drop out of school. She was right. In an almost immediate moment of clarity, I knew that what did not kill me would make me stronger. I got a job working at the Bank of America to earn enough money, together with maximum student loans, to allow me to finish college. I would do whatever it took to pursue the dream inspired by my young father, to become a top notch civil jury trial lawyer.

My father was my role model. He was hard working, calm, kind, and caring. He was a great jury trial lawyer. He taught me, by his actions, that being a good professional and being a good person are equally important. As a child, I recall going to the office with my father. He introduced me to lawyers and staff. I could not help noticing that he asked about and listened to details about the lives of the staff. When the elevator opened at the lobby of his building, he greeted, with warmth and sincere friendship, the man whose job it was to shine shoes. I noticed my father not only called this man by name, but knew the names of his wife and children. The genuine, long term affection between them was evident.

I must have been about twelve years old when my father took me to trial with him. I sat in the courtroom and watched the judge, the jury, and direct and cross examination of witnesses. At the break, the judged invited me into chambers. Everyone, even the court reporter, was male. The only women in the courtroom were on the jury. Undaunted by the absence of any women and apparently

40

oblivious to the challenges that might lie ahead, I left the courtroom that day with the knowledge that I would become the best civil jury trial lawyer I could be. Though the tragedy of my father's very early passing threatened to take away the dream, I remain grateful I was able to hang on to my dream to become an accomplished trial lawyer.

And, as I spoke on that evening of my installation in January 2005, I told the story of my dad, Jacob U. D'Angelo, the trial lawyer, the compassionate human being, who, had he lived just two more months, would have been sworn in as President of the American Board of Trial Advocates, the very same post I was assuming this night, thirty years later. I never imagined I might be able to honor him in such a public way all these years later. The circle of life had come full circle; and, as I battled the emotion of the moment and finished my final comments, I saw my son, Matthew, my husband, Randy, my sisters, my clients, and my friends, standing, applauding, and smiling.

The journey, however challenging, has been consistently filled with passion, intellectual challenges, and commitment. I love the practice of law. Many of the events along the way seem stranger than fiction, but those events will be the subject of another essay. I do know for certain that the profession has given more to me than I could have hoped for. Was it worth it? Absolutely.

B.A., University of California, Santa Barbara, J.D., California Western School of Law and completed last year at Loyola Law School. Donna Melby is a partner at the Los Angeles office of the international law firm, Paul, Hastings, Janofsky & Walker LLP, where she chairs the employment law department. She is a nationally recognized business trial lawyer and was the first woman elected national president of ABOTA (national defense and plaintiff civil trial counsel). She serves on Governor Schwarzenegger's Judicial Selection Advisory Panel and on the Resource Board of the National Association of Women Judges. She has been recognized as one of

California's "Most Talented and Influential Trial Lawyers," as one of the top 100 attorneys in California, and, in addition, one of the 500 best trial lawyers in the U.S. She was featured on The National Law Journal "50 Most Influential Women in America" list that recognizes attorneys who have had a national impact in their legal field and beyond during the last five years.

Fields, Courts, and Leaping High

Stacey R. Preston

The Warm Up

Growing up in Los Angeles, sports were everywhere – college and professional teams to root for and, in school and the nearby YMCAs and recreation centers, so many opportunities to participate. As a young child, I was an enthusiastic ballerina, baton twirler, and roller skater. After developing a fair amount of coordination and strength (but not a whole lot of height), I became smitten with gymnastics.

By junior high, I was a dedicated student of the sport, spending hours each week sweating through gymnastics classes and conditioning at the local YMCA. I was blessed to have a coach who was not only a fine person, but also had the foresight to inspire his young charges to dream about college by taking us to collegiate gymnastics meets where we watched in awe as the older girls performed their routines.

Through years of participating in gymnastics, I honed a variety of useful skills including time management, goal setting, teamwork, dedication, concentration, self-improvement, poise, and

43

resilience. I firmly believe those skills contributed to my achievements in the classroom as well. I was consistently an honors student; and, in my senior year of high school, I was selected captain of the girls' gymnastics team.

During a practice meet just before the start of the competition season of my senior year in high school, I landed awkwardly during the final tumbling pass in my floor exercise routine. A loud pop screamed from my knee as I finished a back flip. I was devastated to learn I had suffered a significant knee injury – an injury that signaled the end of my gymnastics career.

In the fall, I began my undergraduate studies at the University of California, Los Angeles, no longer a gymnast but still an avid student. Being enrolled at a university, with endless opportunities to learn, was exciting. The campus was filled with knowledge, talent, and possibility. UCLA also had a proud tradition of excellence in intercollegiate athletics, and the sporting events on campus were an enriching part of the overall college experience.

Field of Law

Not ready to stop learning after receiving my bachelor's degree, I went directly to law school. Where college had been an all-around amazing experience, law school was different. Much of my work experience prior to starting law school had been teaching gymnastics and working with youngsters as a summer camp counselor. I had quizzed my lawyer cousin at length about the legal field, but I am certain I had never set foot inside a law firm or courtroom before starting law school. It was unfamiliar territory. During my first semester of law school, I questioned whether it was really for me. Nevertheless, I tapped something inside of me – something ingrained through athletics – that allowed me to persevere.

After that first semester, once the newness of being a 1L began to wear off, I found law school much more enjoyable. I grew accustomed to the Socratic Method and being called on in class without volunteering. I was selected to a law journal, first as a staff

44

member and later as the chief production editor. I met a study partner who remains one of my closest friends to this day. Together we survived grueling study sessions, grueling workouts at the Y to stay sane, and a grueling bar exam that, happily, we both passed!

I enjoyed the practice of law – so much so that I practiced for over ten years. I started out working at a well-established litigation firm with over 100 lawyers in Santa Monica, where I gained tremendous experience. I honed my skills as a litigator, learning to write persuasively, argue passionately, and advise logically. I developed as a professional and a person, thanks to wonderful mentors who showed me the way and believed I could be an excellent lawyer.

I eventually joined the ranks of transactional attorneys with a move to the global law firm of Pillsbury Winthrop. After years of experience in litigation, I yearned for the opportunity to help put deals together instead of just litigating them once they fell apart. I was soon working on significant commercial real estate transactions, many of them valued at tens of millions of dollars. I had great clients, and I had great colleagues. I had great mentors who became great friends.

Six years after I became a lawyer, I married one. My husband, Scott, is a litigator; and he likes to tell our friends that in all the years we've been married, he's never won a single argument. Not one. I am certain he made that same joke when we met Eddie Sheldrake at the Wooden Award gala in 2003. The Wooden Award is presented annually to the male and female collegiate basketball players of the year. Eddie had played basketball for Coach John Wooden at UCLA and had gone on to become a prominent and successful businessman and a UCLA Hall of Fame inductee. Eddie and my husband were seated next to each other during the Wooden Award dinner. Eddie's kindness that evening changed our lives.

In the Stands

My interest in the law was outpaced only by my interest in athletics. My husband and I regularly attended college basketball

45

and football games, home and away. We attended college gymnastics meets and NCAA championships. When we did, I often told my husband how rewarding I thought it would be to work in intercollegiate athletics.

Tiring of this refrain and nudging me to pursue my dreams, my husband asked Eddie if he would introduce me to his longtime friend, Dr. Gary Cunningham. Gary is the Director of Athletics at the University of California, Santa Barbara. He is also a fellow UCLA alumnus, a legend in intercollegiate athletics, and a most kind and generous person. Eddie graciously agreed to introduce me to Gary; I had numerous questions to ask him about the field of athletics administration.

When Gary phoned me at my office a few weeks later, I asked him if I could take him to lunch to discuss college athletics administration. His response? "No." For about a half-second, I was crestfallen. And then he continued, "No, I'm going to take you to lunch."

On the Shoulders of Titans

During lunch, I explained to Gary that I was interested in exploring possible opportunities in intercollegiate athletics administration. He advised me to pursue work in an athletics compliance office on a university campus. Since I was a lawyer, this would be a natural transition. The trouble was I already had great clients and worked for a great firm – I wasn't interested in leaving that behind to become a lawyer in an athletics department. I asked him what else might be available for someone with my skills and experience. It turned out there were many opportunities.

The starting point was identifying the skills I had developed as an attorney. Telling someone in another industry you take depositions, argue motions, try cases, or close deals might make you sound like an experienced attorney; but non-lawyers are probably unfamiliar with what those duties entail, and you might not be conveying the breadth and scope of your transferable skills. Boiling down your experience to the fundamentals and giving

46

detailed examples, like writing skills, presentation skills, organizational skills, management skills, analytical skills, research skills, negotiation skills as well as client service, attention to detail, and budget management, can give people outside the legal profession a much better understanding of what you offer.

Once I explained what I actually did as an attorney on a day-to-day basis and articulated why I believed intercollegiate athletics administration would be so rewarding for me, Gary wrote out two lists for me. The first listed jobs in college athletics I might not otherwise have thought of; and the second listed the names of fellow athletics directors and conference commissioners Gary suggested I meet. He understood I was considering a significant move and wanted to help me obtain broad insight and thorough feedback from others in his field so I could make an educated decision about my career path. He also provided me with an industry publication to help me learn more about the field.

With Gary's help, I was introduced to several athletics administrators in the Los Angeles area. I learned that the fields of law and athletics shared a common bond: relationships. Although their schools competed against each other on the courts and fields, these administrators were part of an amiable group with deep mutual respect. During my quest to learn more about the field of athletics administration, Dan Guerrero, the Director of Athletics at UCLA, met with me more than once. Dan gave me honest feedback, clear insight, and good counsel. He shared lessons from his own journey as an athletics administrator, and he reminded me that sometimes you just have to take a leap of faith.

I began to sense that my dream of a rewarding career in intercollegiate athletics could be attainable. After meeting with several athletics administrators, I concluded that: 1) all the athletics professionals I met were genuinely nice people who took great joy in helping others; 2) after gaining insight about the realities of working in intercollegiate athletics, I still felt that the field would be tremendously rewarding, that I would have a lasting passion for it, and that I had unique and valuable skills to offer; and 3) the best way for me to gain experience would be to take an internship shadowing an athletics director to get a full understanding of how an athletics department operates. I felt confident that, given the collective experience of these individuals in the field of athletics administration, from their sturdy shoulders I would have an expansive view of the landscape of the profession and would develop a strong foundation from which to chase my dreams.

The type of internship I envisioned was one that would allow me to rotate through different units within an athletics department, somewhat like a law firm's program for summer associates (two weeks in litigation, two weeks in corporate, two weeks in real estate, and so on). Although no such internship program existed on the campuses I had visited, a number of athletics directors I met offered to craft such an internship if I was willing to volunteer my services during the upcoming academic year.

I had done exhaustive research and was excited about the prospect of a career in athletics administration. Nevertheless, leaving my position as a senior associate at a great firm was not an easy decision. I felt like I was about to step off a cliff. My husband and other family members were incredibly supportive, and my friends told me I was courageous to follow my dreams. Over and over, I kept thinking: how can I do this? After carefully mulling over the pros and cons, in a quiet moment I finally had my answer: how can I not?

A Leap of Faith

I was not one of those unhappy lawyers you read about. Sometimes you simply have to take a leap of faith. At least that's what I told myself when I walked into the managing partner's office at Pillsbury Winthrop and told him I was leaving the firm to take an unpaid internship at Long Beach State University.

He was gracious and supportive. As we discussed my decision to pursue a dream of working in intercollegiate athletics, he told me he understood. He kindly reassured me I was not stepping

48

off a figurative cliff and said, "If you ever change your mind, I'd better be your first phone call."

Leading Off

I selected Long Beach State for my internship because of the experience and temperament of the senior members of the athletics staff, the stature of the athletics program in the Big West Conference, and the assurance I would have opportunities to handle a wide variety of projects (marketing, fundraising, NCAA championships, business, and compliance). In addition, Long Beach State had been selected to host that year's NCAA Division I women's volleyball regional and the following year's championship, and I was particularly excited about working on those events.

The cordial staff gave me a warm welcome and readily included me in their work. I'm sure they didn't know what to make of a lawyer moving into their office for an academic year. The title assigned to me was Special Assistant to the Executive Director of Athletics. I was given business cards, a parking space, and most of all, the opportunity of a lifetime. It was exhilarating to be back on a university campus, in an atmosphere bursting with knowledge, talent, and possibility. The internship was a great experience, and I made some terrific friends.

Field of Athletics

As the end of the academic year approached, I considered the next step in my new career. One job posting that was especially intriguing was for a full-time position at the NCAA national office. I was well qualified for the job. However, it required five years of experience and a move to Indianapolis. On the last day to submit an application, I discussed the job opening with my husband. "Just send your resume," he said. "Make them tell you no. Don't do it for them." I was offered the position approximately one year after first meeting Gary Cunningham for lunch. My husband and I decided to relocate to Indianapolis.

My time at the NCAA has been rewarding. My responsibilities in the branding and communications group center on promoting the eighty-eight NCAA championships and enhancing the championship experiences of student-athletes across the nation. I still manage contracts and make presentations. I still oversee budgets and analyze issues. I utilize so many of the skills I developed as an attorney.

While writing this essay, I received an email requesting my attendance at the NCAA site visit for the next National Collegiate Women's Gymnastics Championships (honestly). I have been assigned to work on that event in the upcoming academic year. Funny where you can land when you leap!

B.A., with honors, University of California, Los Angeles, J.D., Loyola Law School, Los Angeles. Stacey Preston is currently Assistant Director of Brand Strategies and Events at the National Collegiate Athletic Association in Indianapolis, Indiana. She moved to the NCAA from Long Beach State University, where she served as special assistant to the Executive Director of Athletics. Prior to that, she practiced law as a senior associate in the Los Angeles office of Pillsbury Winthrop LLP (now Pillsbury Winthrop Shaw Pittman LLP). She is grateful to her family, friends, and mentors for their eager and absolute support.

Fulfilling Your Destiny

Andrea L. Johnson

Sometimes it takes nearly a lifetime to embrace the destiny that God meant for you, even though you may see it as a child or articulate it as an adult. Perhaps that is why life is called a journey.

When I was a young girl of eleven, I went to visit my paternal grandmother in Nashville, Tennessee, for two weeks as I had done every summer since infancy. Grandma Nerva was a high school history teacher, and she had the summers off from teaching. It was not uncommon for some of her students to be over at the house visiting. My grandmother would hold court, telling stories of days past and providing advice. She would feed them and clothe them, if necessary. She even let one of her students live in the guest unit over the garage. I was fascinated by the reverence and fondness they felt for her, holding on to her every word. But, it also made me jealous. The bond with her students was independent of me and the family, and neither I nor anyone else could break it. One afternoon I was annoyed that a couple of her students were at the house. I pouted all day. After they left, I asked her why she spent so much time with them or had them around.

Grandma Nerva pulled me close and said, "You are my only granddaughter, and I love you dearly. Whatever I have will be yours one day. These are my students. They are not taking me from you, but I am their teacher. They need me in a special way, and you have to understand that I will be there for them."

She paused, cocked her head to the side, looking intently at my bowed head, waiting for some affirmation that I understood. Slowly, ashamed, I looked up and nodded; but I still couldn't understand how people who were not family could love and adore her as I did. I watched her interact with her students the rest of the summer. She had a special gift to inspire learning in young people. My jealousy turned to awe; and I vowed to myself that if I ever taught, I wanted my students to feel about me the way my grandmother's students felt about her.

I was reminded of that summer a couple of years ago when one of my student's parents approached me after a graduation commencement ceremony at the law school where I teach. "It's amazing to me how much my daughter adores you." I smiled and humbly said, "I'm glad." I had fulfilled my destiny by becoming a teacher like my grandmother.

I am a fifth generation college graduate and fourth generation educator. Whatever our avocation, education was always stressed in my family and learning took place whenever we came together. My great, great grandmother graduated in 1872 from Fisk University in Nashville, Tennessee, and taught music. My grandfather was the dean of men and the football coach at Fisk during the 1940s, where every other member of my immediate family, except me, went to college. Education, self-sufficiency, humility, good manners, and the importance of family were values handed down through the generations and allowed my family to thrive in the South in spite of being Black and middle class at the height of Jim Crow violence.

My father, a practicing dentist and very active in the community, was a Southern gentlemen who treated everyone with respect. He assumed I would get married and raise a family, as the other women in the family had done. But he believed I had a gift of intellect that needed to be nurtured and challenged. After being elected the first Black chairman of the board of Cuyahoga Community College in Cleveland, Ohio, my father made it clear he

52

wanted me to learn how to think "like a man," and use my brain. "I want you to feel comfortable in the boardroom, as well as on the street."

My mother, a junior high math teacher before retiring to raise her kids, returned to academia after we were grown. She retired as vice president of student affairs at Case Western Reserve. She taught me how to be true to myself as a woman with sex-appeal, despite often being the first or only woman, African-American, or both.

Despite a rich tradition in education, I never had a desire to teach. Being so close to it,   I wanted to be more than a teacher, or do more, although I wasn't sure why or what. Grandma Nerva taught me, "If you want to have autonomy in your life, you have to control something that is critical to the community: real estate, public works, communication, transportation, or security."

I loved the arts: painting, sculpting, dancing, and writing poetry. I strived when I was being creative. I spent a lot of time in my head and was perceived as being "different," a "free spirit," or "out-of-the-box." After attending Harvard Law School and working for a Wall Street firm, I did well as an entrepreneur in communications and real estate.

Despite my success, I discovered I did not like the person I had become. I was a classic, Type A personality, with all of the associated intensity and stress from competing in tough, traditionally male environments: corporate tax, commercial development, and broadcasting. It was hard to compete. I often felt that everyone was lined up for a "pissing" match, and I was left scratching my head trying to figure out how to compete because I lacked the right equipment. The experiences taught me how to be effective but made me hard and rigid.

I asked my father for advice. He said, "I realize you have worked hard, but at the end of the day, if you've got everything you're striving for, would you still want it." When I realized my answer was no, I walked away from all of it. I struggled not to see my decision as a failure or defeat but a conscious choice to like myself and make myself happy. I started teaching to clear my head and to reinforce my legal skills. In the back of my mind, however, I was still determined to do something more.

At first, I felt I had a knack for teaching. Then I realized how challenging it was to be a "good" teacher and struggled to understand how to be effective at making sure students actually learned something. To retain some creativity, I chose to focus on using technology by developing a web-based law curriculum and the first distance-learning class at a U.S. law school. After sixteen plus years teaching law, I feel I am doing something well and right. And I like myself and the person I have become.

I am filled with a satisfaction I have never known before. And the joy is that my students have responded to me with an appreciation, codependency, and fondness that warms my heart. On the last day of class, I tell my students, "You will always be a student of mine, and I will be there for you. I may not like or approve of what you do, but I will not turn my back." I hood many of them at graduation. After giving them that last hug, I look into their eyes and smile, knowing we are bound for life. I know deep in my heart that my grandmother would be pleased because I have carried the "gift of teaching" forward.

Andrea Johnson is a fifth generation college graduate and a fourth generation educator. She is a tenured professor at California Western School of Law and Director of the Telecommunications and Intellectual Property Center. After graduating from Howard University and Harvard Law School, she worked for a Wall Street firm. As a law professor, she focuses on the use of technology. In 1996, she taught the first distance-learning class at a U.S. law school linking sites using the Internet and videoconferencing. She develops and produces a web-based curriculum called "Cyber Workbooks." She was a Carnegie Scholar and served on President Clinton's Transition Team for Science, Space, and Technology.

How Do They Live?

Ellen J. Dannin

After I finished a federal judicial clerkship, I became a trial attorney in the Detroit region of the National Labor Relations Board. People took their time calling me back. I was no longer on the sidelines. I was in the center of people's lives. I had to go out of the office and investigate cases. That meant meeting with people whose lives had been torn apart, usually because they had tried to organize a union, something that is perfectly legal. To put their lives back together, I had to find witnesses who would then be risking their jobs to protect a co-worker. Asking people to forsake the security of their anonymity and noninvolvement was asking a great deal.

Over the years, I investigated and prepped too many cases to remember. In nearly every one of them, I had to ask ordinary people to be courageous, selfless, heedless of their own self-interest. Asking people to risk their jobs, their livelihood, their families was asking for courage and selflessness so great I am awed that so many said yes with no hesitation. They did what I asked out of motives of friendship, out of a sense of justice, because they felt someone they worked with had been wronged. These people taught me there is a huge reservoir of goodness, honor, and morality in ordinary people. These were people who were not directly affected and who could easily have stayed uninvolved. Some of them asked what would protect them from being treated the way Big Red or Joe or Mary Ellen was – the ones who had been fired – if they stuck their necks out.

It was a serious question I tried to answer as truthfully as possible. All the time I was consumed with fear of the consequences if I missed the nuances. I was afraid they would decide I was asking far too much and refuse to help. If they refused to help, then how would I prove the case, how would I do my job, how would a wrong be righted?

At the same time, I had to tell them I could not guarantee them that if they cooperated with the government, they would walk away unscathed. If I was not honest, if I did not make it clear there certainly were risks, they might decide to come forward and suffer consequences they were unprepared for. I did not want their blood on my hands. But I also wanted them to feel compelled to do the right thing, to live up to a duty that would prompt them to do something brave and crazy and humane.

You see, even though I may have looked like a middle-class government lawyer, at that time I had just crawled out of poverty. Not too far under my skin, I was the people sitting on the other side of the table or on the other end of the phone line. Being plunged into poverty wasn't an abstraction for me, yet it was a consequence that could come about for the people I was talking to and because I was talking to them.

Looked at one way, my childhood was a bucolic ideal. I grew up as a child in a town of about 1,000 in rural Ohio. My mother was home most of the time. If my little brother or sister or I walked two blocks north of our house, past the Civil War cemetery, we were in the country. On Church Street there was a Lutheran, Baptist, Methodist, and then around the corner, a Catholic Church. Not only did everyone know everyone else, we had grown up together. So had our parents and our grandparents. We walked to our local public school; and in this school and in this town, I was shaped. It was there I learned the art of working-class, self-deprecating humor.

But there was a lot missing from this seemingly idyllic picture. My father, a doctor, had deserted us when I was five years old. Suddenly, we were poor. My mother tried to work; but it was hard in that day, as it is now, for a single mother with three small children to find any work, let alone work that paid enough to support us.

Being poor is going to school in old wilted clothes that never fit right and that make the child ashamed. It is eating oatmeal for a week at a time, except for the school lunch. We were rural poor, so we planted seeds and had a garden. We did the rural equivalent of finding food in the garbage; we scavenged in the woods, cut asparagus from the old neglected Civil War cemetery, picked strawberries from along the railroad tracks. Often we only survived because of the charity of relatives and others.

The school I attended was a model of educating children on the cheap. It had two sorts of teachers. The young ones were recruited teachers fresh out of teacher's college from poor states like West Virginia who thought the lower than average salary was pretty good in comparison to what was offered at home. They would come, get some experience, and then leave after a year or two for jobs that paid a living wage. The older teachers had not gone to college, just a few months education past high school. My fourth grade teacher had taught my grandfather, my mother, and all my aunts. The school was old, crumbling, and dreary. You had to be careful sitting in the seats or you would get splinters. In the town's high school, the two biggest clubs were Future Farmers of America and Future Homemakers of America.

For all this, I was lucky in many ways because I found a way to escape from the misery and confinement of my life – books. My mother loved to read, and I loved to read. I haunted the library. I read through the encyclopedia before I was ten. In fifth grade, I was so far ahead of my class that my teacher could not figure out what to do with me, so she told me to spend the day on the playground and not to get into trouble. With teachers, as with many things, you get what you pay for. Had I been in a decent school, the kind found in wealthier suburbs, I would not have been outside the school, left to pick up what I could, but would have been given enrichment classes.

One year, just before school was to start, the most terrible and most wonderful event in my life occurred – the house we lived in burned down. We left the smoking ashes and moved fifteen miles away to a slightly larger town that was actually worlds away. The people of this town valued education and funded their schools adequately. My new school taught foreign languages and had a language lab. There was music and drama. It had wonderful creative teachers with master's degrees. There were clubs and all sorts of extra-curricular activities. It was clean and beautiful with even some special touches that no corner-cutting builder would have put in, but there they were. This was a place built by people who loved and cherished children, and no one could doubt it.

The first few months were miserable for me. I went from being the smartest student in school to struggling because I was far behind. Every minute it was painfully obvious that my education had been incomplete, inadequate, deficient. But I was encouraged and nurtured by my teachers. Slowly I learned. By the end of the first year, I became and remained a straight A student and the only child in the advanced classes whose parents did not belong to the country club, who wore used, hand-me-down clothing, who lived in a part of town none of them had ever seen, in a rundown house just across from the railroad tracks. I felt different and excluded from most of the social life there. But because there was support for that school and because the school supported me, I had and now have so much.

By the standards of today, I deserved nothing. My father could have paid to support me but didn't. My mother was depressed and even dysfunctional at times. But the public schools didn't punish me for their failings. They took me as I was. They educated me. They made me into a productive member of this society. But I was lucky. How many children whose parents slip into poverty find good fortune in a house burning down or have a parent who, despite other shortcomings, is able to nurture the skills

58

that end up being a ticket to the middle class? There is just no guarantee that anyone who suffered repercussions from cooperating in my work would come out as well as I did.

So what do I do when I reach that point at which I am asked if it is dangerous to help in a case? I tell them there are laws on the books to protect them in the event of retaliation. But I also explain there are laws on the books that say don't kill other people, but somehow people keep getting killed. I tell them there are bad people in the world who will do whatever they want regardless of laws and punishments. But I tell them laws cannot be effective unless people have the courage and compassion for others to come forward, to stand up. I tell them they have rights now only because others stood up and took risks, and the only way to ensure we all have rights is to do the same, to pay others back for what they did for us – even though they did not even know us.

I understood but was disappointed when some decided they just could not come forward. But so few decided to step aside. More often, these very ordinary people overcame their fears to cooperate in our effort to get at the truth and enforce the laws. These people are the real heroes of our democracy, and they let me into their lives.

Years may have passed, but I can still picture that dingy union hall in Madison Heights filled with folding chairs and tables, witnesses lined up in the waiting room, their children crawling on the floor or over their laps. Once we had finished, they packed the kids into the car and hurried over to the factory where the second shift was starting, leaving the kids in the car to be driven home by the other parent who would hurry to the car once the first shift ended. Some work the arrangement on the third and first shift, packing sleepy babies into warm clothes for that cold dawn drive to the plant and the parking lot exchange. They do this for less and less money each year. Minimum wage, a dollar above minimum wage, dirty jobs, no hope.

I have been to their houses paid for by what these wages afford. The houses are small, with old wooden floors that wave and creak. Or they are made of chipped linoleum. Or ragged, stained pieces of carpet. The niches, televisions, walls are all decorated with bright knickknacks. They live on top of one another. In some houses, there is filth and a stench. In some, I move piles of dirty dishes to find a spot to write my notes and take their statements. In others, there is order, cleanliness, evidence of thinking about more than mere existence. Organic Gardening seems to have universal appeal.

Some of them tell me their hopes for the future. Some of them tell me about their children. Some of them tell me of their despair that they can ever live in dignity or even just live. They describe where they work, the waste of time and materials, the lack of caring on the part of the owners. They shake their heads as they outline how to make things more efficient, make more money. I have heard the owners point to the shop floor and say, "You see all those people out there? They're just trash." This is the trash whose work paid for the expensive cars I saw parked in the owner's reserved spot.

I have been to homes these bosses will never visit. And if they ever did, they would assume this is all these people deserve. A once yearly company picnic. Some games and superficial conversations ought to do it in the camaraderie department.

I wonder: would it make any difference in the way bargaining is conducted, policies implemented, if the rich and powerful could see and know what I have seen and known? What about the judges on their benches, especially the court of appeals judges, who see nothing but what has been cauterized and sterilized, reduced to legalities? What can help them see over, through, and into the blood that flows just below the surface of the briefs and transcripts? To be a good trial lawyer you must be an exquisitely sensitive person. You must be responsive to your witnesses, to the other side's witnesses, to nuances of gesture and expression, to the probabilities of situations, to how others – and especially the judge – will view your case and the other side's case.

At the same time, you must be self-confident and possess an unwavering certainty in the rightness of what you do. You must be willing to run over other people, including your witnesses, for the sake of the case. You must be confident that if they don't want to participate, too bad. They are the chess pieces you need to move around the board to win. But, be too single-minded, and you will miss important issues. Go a bit farther along the continuum, and you become so boorish no one will want you around let alone be persuaded by what you have to say.

But too much sensitivity is paralyzing. Worry too much about your witnesses and how they are affected by the process, and you will be paralyzed, unable to do anyone any good. At best, you spend your time oscillating between the extremes, trying to pick the right mode for each moment. At worst, it eats you up.

As for me, these days I don't try cases. I try to teach.

Ellen Dannin is Professor of Law at Pennsylvania State University Dickinson School of Law. She is the author of Taking Back the Workers' Law – How to Fight the Assault on Labor Rights (2006). She has been a trial attorney for the U.S. National Labor Relations Board. Professor Dannin has lived in New Zealand as a scholar in residence. She taught at California Western School of Law, Wayne State University, University of Michigan, and University of Massachusetts. B.A., J.D., University of Michigan.

I Never Wanted to Be a Lawyer

Julia A. Cline

"Our modern society tends to glamorize the working mother, while the impression is given that any woman can be a housewife. When a girl is married, she automatically becomes a housewife, but it may take special qualifications to work outside the home."
Christian Fellowship Society, Ebenezer Church, Leota, Minnesota, 1977.

I never wanted to be a lawyer. I never dreamed of wearing a blue (or black) suit, sensible shoes, and saying "Yes, your honor." I never dreamed of writing perfectly footnoted and cited motions about mundane issues. I dreamt of something more bohemian, like acting or psychology. My acting career was over at a very young age when I was cast as a blind girl in the story of Helen Keller and wore my glasses on stage. As to psychology, I did graduate with a psychology degree which led me to my first career, retail. Becoming a lawyer was born out of my desire, drum role please, to have discussions with my husband in which I was clearly correct on every issue.

My husband, who had always dreamt of being a lawyer, was in his first year of law school when I realized I could no longer respond to his diatribes regarding the Learned Hand theory or the causes of actions for a surgery resulting in a hairy hand. I, in fact, knew nothing about a smart hand or a hairy hand. I decided I needed to educate myself, by going hugely in debt, in order to save my marriage. It turned out I actually had a knack for the law and was able to graduate and get a job with the federal government.

I showed up to my job in my blue suit for the first day of work unprepared for the human challenges before me. I was hired at the same time as another woman. On our first day of work, an older male colleague greeted us by asking, "Why did they hire two married females who are just going to get pregnant and leave?" Not knowing how to respond, we both stared at him with our mouths gaping wondering what century we had stumbled into and how do we get out of here. Even though his comment was insensitive and rude, it turned out to be true – all except the part about both of us leaving. We are both proud mothers of two girls, and I'm still working for the federal government.

There were many days, especially during my first couple years on the job, when I cried in the morning before going to work and wished that the lottery fairy would visit me. When pregnant with my first child, I was prevented from leaving court to get lunch because, by God, the judge was going to finish the case with or without me. I have also found the idea of making accommodations for working parents is a theory that works only when those accommodations make your life more difficult without affecting anyone else in the office. My hope for those young lawyers just entering the field is that they will be surrounded by more and more individuals, both men and women, who themselves have juggled family and work in their legal careers.

I was one of those people who said that children would not affect my career or lifestyle. At the time I had my first child, I was working full-time and sitting on the boards of two nonprofit organizations. I remember standing through meetings with my first

64

child in a Baby Bjorn, just hoping and praying that my bouncing and swaying would keep her quiet long enough to get through the meeting. At the time of my second child's birth, I was president of two boards. Now I'm on no boards and find I still cannot do it all. The most important phrase I have learned is "sorry, I don't have time...two children under five." This works in the majority of circumstances.

I have, for the past couple years, continued only one outside activity. I have had the pleasure of meeting young lawyers by teaching Negotiation at the local law school. This semester I asked them, in preparation for writing this article, "What is so difficult about being a lawyer?" As we talked about the responsibilities of and pressures on lawyers, we started to discuss why lawyers have a higher than normal rate of suicide and substance abuse. One of the conclusions we came to is, as lawyers, we are reluctant to reach out to others for help or for advice. We are lawyers, and we know all the answers. In fact, we know some answers to a few questions in a very narrow area of law.

The best resources for surviving as a lawyer are lawyer friends you can call when you need a little lift and free therapy (because you can only whine for so long about a case to your significant others before they get that glazed look and start picking their teeth while looking up at the sky). This brings me to the next question presented to me by my students, "Would you recommend being married to a lawyer?" The answer, I told them, was sometimes yes and sometimes no.

For example, on a recent drive into work together, I found myself cross-examining my husband about why he had chosen this given route to work and why he was in the left lane and unable to find the gas. After arriving at work and not talking to each other, I reluctantly text messaged him while I was in court. I apologized for questioning him on the ride into work. His answer text messaged back from his deposition was "so stipulated." The good thing about being married to a lawyer – and my husband – is he understands that on some days, he needs to do 100% of the parenting and on

65

some days I can do 100% of the parenting. This sharing works most of the time until you reach one of those days when both of you need time off.

Finally, the hardest thing about being a mom and a lawyer is the little things. These little things took me totally by surprise. On most mornings, I get to work well before my daughters have lifted their little bed heads from the pillow. I feel guilty I was not there to greet them in the morning with a kiss and hug. My husband tells me they ask for me in the morning (he may be lying about this point, but I choose to believe him) and understand I've already left for work. I feel horrible I have no idea what they were wearing or if their hair was in ponytails or braids. I feel as if I have abandoned them every day to go out in the world and work in my navy blue suit. While I feel the longing and guilt of missing some moments of their lives, I also know that I have been given the opportunity and skills to be a lawyer. Frankly, I am a pretty good housewife too!

B.A., Hope College, J.D., California Western School of Law, cum laude. Julia Cline "works" as a full time wife and mother of two, full time federal litigator, and part-time law professor teaching Negotiation. She was president of the California Western alumni board of directors. For years, she has coached trial teams.

Latina in Law

Gloria L. Sandrino

I am an immigrant! Not an illegal immigrant – but an immigrant none the less. I arrived in the United States in 1967 with my mother, grandmother, and sister. My father had spoken against the Castro regime and was sentenced to four years in prison. So my courageous mother left her homeland, the beautiful island of Cuba, and came to the United States to provide a better life for her girls. She spoke no English and had no money – but with two Ph.D.s, she knew she would make it.

My early memories of America are not pleasant ones. As an Afro-Cuban (a Black Latina), I was shocked with the blatant racism that plagued American society. As all Cubans who immigrated to the United States, we had to live with our "sponsors." Our sponsors, distant relatives of my father, lived in Dayton, Ohio. In the late 1960s, Dayton was a hot-bed of racial conflict, with daily riots and protests. I often asked my mother, "Is this better than communism?" Her reply was always the same, "No society is perfect, but in America anyone can get an education. And an education is the ticket to success."

Education was a priority in our household. My mother and grandmother didn't allow us to do anything but focus on learning English. My sister and I were encouraged to read all the time. There

67

was no television allowed during the school week, just trips to the local library. Little by little, my sister and I learned English and adapted to our new "home."

Indeed, my mother's education served us well. Within two years, she was able to learn English, take verbal tests to prove she indeed had two advanced degrees, and secure a job as a bilingual teacher. We settled into a comfortable middle class life. The most important lesson for my sister and me was that an education was the only path to success – for financial success and for personal success.

My father came to the United States in 1971. The U.S. government had asked Castro for the release of political prisoners for humanitarian reasons, and my father was one of those prisoners. I remember going to the airport to pick him up, and his first words were, "I am so glad to have the chance to give my girls a better life."

My father and mother worked very hard so my sister and I could have a great education and life experiences. They worked several jobs in order to afford to send us to private school, have music lessons, and travel abroad. It was important to them for us to assimilate while at the same time maintaining a sense of our language and culture. At home, we always spoke Spanish and read Spanish novels to perfect our understanding of our mother tongue.

After receiving my law degree from Harvard Law School, I went to work at a large firm on Wall Street. At twenty-three, I was making more money than my mother (with two Ph.D.s) had ever made. I was eager and determined to make partner. I specifically asked the hiring partner in my interview if making partner was a viable option. He nodded, but I later discovered the answer was "probably not." I had three strikes against me: Latina, woman, and Black.

I did well at the law firm. I was a corporate attorney doing mergers and acquisitions, initial public offerings, and securities regulation. I loved my job. Although I had no personal life (I worked seven days a week, eleven to thirteen hours a day), I really enjoyed my work and my clients. In my mind, I was on partnership track.

An African-American male lawyer in my department became my mentor. Two years my senior, he had an undergraduate and law degree from Stanford, as well as an M.B.A. He was smart, well-connected, and worked on the firm's biggest deals. The year he was up for partner, the minority attorneys at the firm (seven of seven hundred in the New York office) were planning a huge party. If he made it (and we had no doubts he would), he would be the first minority partner in that firm's history.

He did not make it. He did not lose the vote; his name was never submitted for a vote. The head partner of the corporate department (the firm's biggest department) felt the firm's clients were not ready for a "partner of color." That was the explanation given to us. It was not his work, his legal experience, his writing ability – it was his color! This was not 1967 – it was 1987.

I thought back to my days in Dayton – with the riots and the protests. At least the racism was blatant. I could see it in people's eyes and actions. The law firm racism was masked with assertions such as, "Of course partnership is a viable option." Shortly after, I left the firm.

I decided to move to Miami, Florida, home of the largest population of Cubans in the United States. I wanted to feel part of a "majority." While in Miami, I worked for a branch office of a large New York law firm. While Cubans dominated the popular culture in Miami, the legal world was still male and white. The same issues of race and gender that existed in New York were part of the law firm life in Miami. For example, my secretary, a young Cuban girl, spoke to me in Spanish when things became hectic at the law firm. One day, a corporate partner overheard her and started to yell at her, "This is an English only law firm!"

I decided to leave law practice for teaching. Teaching law has allowed me to explore issues of race, ethnicity and gender – both in the classroom and in my scholarship. In this twenty-first century, the politics of racial articulation is sublimated in the proxy languages of "culture," "underclass," and "people of color." Law firms and corporate America are still struggling with issues of diversity and attracting and retaining attorneys of color. Change always proceeds unevenly. In my mind, the only truism is that education is the key to success.

In my personal life, I still embrace the "celebration" of the mixture of races. My husband is Jewish, and our three children are being raised Jewish (with a huge dose of Spanish and Latino culture).

B.A., Rutgers University, Phi Beta Kappa, J.D., Harvard Law School. Gloria Sandrino is a native of Cuba, practiced corporate law in Miami with Weil, Gotshal, & Manger, and in New York at Fried, Frank, Harris, Shriver & Jacobson LLP and at Kelley Drye & Warren LLP. She worked as a project organizer with the Cuban Refugee Settlement Program. She has taught at California Western School of Law since 1991 (Business Organizations, Business Planning, International Finance, International Business Transactions, and Latinos/as and the Law). She is the married mother of three.

Learning to Leave It at Work

Margo L. Lewis

I remember the first time I was asked the question: what do you want to be when you grow up? I was ten years old and in the fourth grade. This was also the year the answer to that question became clear to me. I lived with my mom, dad, and older brother on 54th Avenue in Moline, Illinois. Each day on my walk home from school, my brother and I would pass an amazing white house with white pillars, a red door, and a huge tree in the front yard. I didn't know who lived in that house, but I was about to find out.

Mrs. Thoman, my fourth grade teacher, instructed each of us in her class to keep a tree diary for the entire school year. It was obvious to me that the tree I would choose would be the one in the front yard of the big white house. My mother bought me a notebook for my journal, and I set out to meet the owner of the house. After all, I would be spending a great deal of time in the front yard studying the big tree. When I knocked on the red door, a tall man answered. He was dressed in a beautiful blue suit with a white shirt and striped tie. I introduced myself and told him I lived down the street. I told him about the tree diary my teacher had assigned and

71

asked if I could study his tree. The man told me his name was Denny, and he told me that is what I should call him. No adults had ever insisted I call them by their first names. Denny informed me he would call me by my first name, and we began talking about my school project. Denny would come outside and join me occasionally when I was studying his tree, and we would visit. Then one day it happened. Denny told me he was a lawyer. I didn't really know what that was or what it meant, but knew I had to be a lawyer.

At age ten, I chose my career, and this decision would never change. I went home to tell my mom, and she agreed I should be a lawyer. I asked my mom how to be a lawyer and what I needed to do. She told me she knew I would need to do really well in school and study very hard, but we agreed it was best to write a letter to a law school to find out for sure. Together, my mom and I decided I would write to Harvard Law School. It took me several attempts to create the perfect letter. Once I was satisfied, I had Denny review it. Within a few weeks, Harvard Law School responded to my letter; and the path for my career was paved.

Being fully aware of the academic requirements for law school, I became a straight A student from that point forward. In high school, I first experienced the "real" legal stuff. My mom and dad were getting a divorce; and the process, mostly the part that involved me, was very interesting. I was fifteen years old, I knew what I wanted, but nobody asked me what was best for me.

I went on to attend college at the University of Iowa and proudly designated myself a pre-law major. Upon graduation from college, I packed my little car, my graduation gift, and set out for San Diego, California. I had been admitted to California Western School of Law, and I had my mother's unwavering support. I graduated law school and spent the summer of 1992 studying for the California Bar Exam, which I passed in fall 1992. The only real problem I faced after achieving this life-long goal was that there were no jobs to be found in San Diego.

It was time to implement Plan B, but what the heck was Plan B? In 1992, you either left San Diego, got lucky with a job offer from

72

a summer law clerking position, or hung out your own shingle. The reality was I was never leaving sunny San Diego, and I did not want to rely on luck; therefore, I started my own firm on December 15, 1992. I went to the lawyer I clerked for during law school and asked for advice. He was a sole practitioner and did not need full time help but agreed I could trade him time for office space. I worked twenty hours per week, or as many hours as he needed, and the Law Office of Margo L. Lewis was created.

My office was in a high-rise building in downtown San Diego. I purchased a computer, printer, supplies, and the Rutter Group books on the practice of family law. My interest in this area had been sparked back in high school. I was intent on working with those teen-age kids, like myself, who had opinions during a divorce, but were never asked. I arrived at work each day at 7:30 a.m. and remained in my office until 6:00 p.m. I spent my days waiting for the telephone to ring, reading law books, and observing attorneys in court.

Within weeks, I had my first few clients. I received minimal retainers, and my hourly rate was a mere $110 per hour. The day came for my first court appearance, and I could not have been more ready or more excited. I appeared at the Superior Court on time in my favorite navy blue suit and sat in the jury box waiting for the judge. The judge called our case and indicated we needed to see him in chambers. Not familiar with this process, I naively followed opposing counsel to the judge's chambers.

The judge, who will remain nameless to this day, looked at me and sighed. He proceeded to ask me, "What's a pretty young gal like you doing in a court room? Are you sure you just don't want to sell something?" I was speechless, as was the male attorney sitting next to me. I gathered my things and stood up with as much poise as I could muster and thanked him for his concern, but assured him I was certain of my career choice. We left chambers, and we appeared in court before this same judge. To this day, I am unsure what I said or how I said it, but my request was denied without any explanation from the judge. As I walked back to my office, there was a brief moment where I questioned my choice to pursue law.

However, since I enjoy a good challenge, I continued to develop my private practice over the next few years. I learned various types of law and took on civil, criminal, and family law cases to keep myself busy, and more importantly, to pay the bills. It only took a few civil cases with male colleagues referring to me as "honey," "sweetheart," and even "bitch" on one occasion, to figure out civil litigation was not my thing.

The next couple years passed like a blur, and my family law practice continued to grow. I had developed a solid reputation. Before I knew it, I was turning away cases because I was too busy. I became familiar with the bench and the bar and began participating in legal groups and committees. The Family Law Bar was a group of men and woman who came together to assist good people going through the worst times in their lives. The bench was also very active with the bar and took a real interest in the rules, activities, and committees that involved family law.

Eventually, I obtained mentors in family law who allowed me to call on them with questions. I relied on their integrity and found that many of them were very willing to help out "young" attorneys. I recall a family law attorney during my first year of practice who gave me important advice I follow to this day. She told me "never take this stuff home with you, and remember it's their life." To this day, I see her in court and thank her under my breath for that one simple piece of advice.

In 1996, I met my law partner, David, while in the courtroom. He was a new attorney, young and equally as energetic as I. We became immediate friends and started our legal partnership within a year. We rented space from a big civil law firm in downtown San Diego and set out to decide who would be first on the letterhead. Being a creative guy with an enormous ego, somewhat like myself, we spent a Friday night having margaritas and asked the first twenty-five people in the bar which firm name sounded better. With an astounding twenty-four to one vote, our firm was born with my name leading the way.

I was thirty and in a profession I really enjoyed. I spent each day with a friend and colleague. We worked long hours, learned together, struggled with cases, laughed, and almost daily, fought like siblings. We shared the joys of our lucrative months and the stress associated with the not-so-busy times. Dave and I shared an interest in the children caught up in the system and pursued work as minors' counsel.

In 1999, things started to change; our little firm was growing. We expanded our partnership in 2000. Two other family law attorneys, Peggy and Erik, mother and son, rented space in our suite. The four of us developed a strong friendship and sought advice from each other regularly. I had known and worked with Peggy in prior years, and I was impressed with the way she treated me when I was a new attorney. Unlike many others, Peggy treated me like a professional and did not take advantage of my limited knowledge. Instead she helped to educate me. I also try to educate and mentor new attorneys in practice.

The four of us created a family law firm in January 2000. We each had motives and reasons for entering into our partnership: for career, for family, and for me, it was so I could have it all. I became a Certified Family Law Specialist in the State of California. In 2001, I gave birth to my daughter, Peyton.

My partners had agreed I would take ten weeks away from work to be a mom without the burdens of a family law practice. Two years later, I became a mother for the second time with the birth of my son, Pacey. My partners allowed me another ten weeks, "vacation time" as David and Erik would jokingly describe it, to take care of my second baby. After I returned to work, I wondered how I could balance work with my desire to be a mom. I could never have imagined the level of guilt I felt walking out the door each morning to do a job I loved. I recall two male judges asking me if I would return to work now that I was a mother. I was shocked by the question, but not as shocked as they were when I told them I would be maintaining a full time practice. I never doubted I could have both. However, the most significant part of my identity had changed from lawyer to mother.

I had it all, so I thought. I was juggling a full time legal practice and being a full time mother who was unwilling to give up any of my children's first experiences. I modified my work week to get five days of billable time into a four-day work week to have three days with my children. I would race home any time our nanny indicated a sickness or a milestone was about to happen. I was there for their first steps, first words, first teeth, and the practice survived. I was under extreme pressure as the provider of our family and, as could be predicted, something had to give. In 2005, I realized my marriage was the one thing that could not survive. I had spent so many years giving advice on divorce that my own failure in this area was hard to handle.

I was now living my biggest fear: a single career mom with two toddlers. I knew I would not let my children down, but things would be difficult. I turned to the resources I had developed after years of family law practice. It was amazing to find the level of support I received from attorneys, psychologists, and friends I had made in this profession. I was grateful to have a career I could bury myself in and not become overwhelmed by my personal life.

I now practice in an area of law I have personally experienced for myself. I admit it is difficult to pull myself out of the situation and take the advice I have been giving to clients in the same spot. The level of insight I have gained in representing children after having children is indescribable. My life experiences have allowed me to see divorce through the eyes of a teenager, as well as a wife and mother. I have true compassion for the children and parents who have experienced the tragedy of divorce. However, I always remember that invaluable advice – "it is not my life," and "leave it at work."

This year has been eventful for me personally and professionally. I have accomplished lifelong personal goals such as running the New York marathon. I have learned to juggle being a single mom with being a career woman. I have found that it's hard, but not impossible. Our little family law firm has expanded from five attorneys to nine attorneys with my law clerk waiting to take the bar exam. The challenges of law are present every day, and that is why we continue to call it a practice.

B.A., University of Iowa, J.D., California Western School of Law. Margo Lewis is a Certified Family Law Specialist, State Bar of California, and a partner at Moore, Lewis, Schulman & Moore, APC. She was named one of the top San Diego Family Law attorneys by the San Diego Daily Transcript in 2006 and 2007. Her volunteer activities include: executive committee chair elect, Certified Family Law Specialists, State of California; chair, Certified Family Law Specialists, Bar Association of North San Diego County; and appointed minor's counsel. She was named a Southern California Super Lawyer – San Diego 2007.

Life in the Ladies' Lane

Laurie L. Levenson

When I had my first child, I lost my position, title, office, secretary, furniture, and, worst of all, my parking spot at the U.S. Attorney's Office. And, there wasn't a darn thing I could do about it.

I started as a prosecutor before I was married. As a single woman, I would work my kishkes out for my job and I did. I loved being a trial lawyer. It was "show time." Five foot one inches and young, my appearance made defense counsel underestimate my abilities and commitment to the cause. Judges tended to set them straight. I recall that golden moment when Judge Laughlin Waters, the tough but fatherly federal judge who was absolutely devoted to his own daughters, corrected a defense lawyer who had called me "Honey." He said, "If you knew Ms. Levenson better, you would never call her that." Little did he know that my nickname in the office was more akin to "Bitch Goddess."

So, for seven years, I tried cases with all the vigor in my body. I put up with sexist judges (you know a judge is a sexist when he comments on your stockings, asks you to wear your knit dress for trial, or asks you why you are just sitting on your "twat" during a hearing – all of which happened to me); long, long hours; men with less seniority and talent getting promotions ahead of me; and assignment to cases that others had rejected. Most of the time, it was still good. What made it good was the amazing cadre of women in the office who stood by me every step of the way. The ladies got me through. It has been twenty-five years, and we still stand by one another. Known as the "bund" or "Oy Luck Club," we have regular dinners to celebrate each other's birthdays and life events. Twelve super-successful women (nine of the twelve are judges) who owe their sanity to one another.

After seven years as a federal prosecutor, I had risen to the upper echelons of the office. I was the "academic" type, so I became Chief of Appeals. I read every brief going out of the office, edited them, dealt with bruised egos, and tried to tone down the macho men who I knew were about to be eaten alive by the Ninth Circuit because of their show of bravado during trial. I was respected and the job was great.

But then came the baby. When I was pregnant with my first child, I worked until one and one half hours before my son was born. The week before, I had been in an eleven-defendant trial. The judge was so nervous having this overdue mother in his courtroom that he asked his clerk to cover the furniture with plastic. That case ultimately went away as I made the point to defense counsel that no juror votes against motherhood. Although I had been in trial the week before, it was habeas corpus that brought on labor.

My son, Solomon ("Solly") the wise, was born. Within a few weeks of having the baby, I stood again in the back of a federal courtroom nursing him (believe me, this isn't done much in federal court) and handing him off to an F.B.I. agent so I could argue a case. It was then and there that I rethought my idea of skipping maternity leave. Instead, I decided to take four months off so I could feed and bond with the little guy and make my body look human again.

When I returned to the office, my job was not waiting for me. Instead, I was shuttled to another position. The corner office was gone, furniture gone, secretary gone. I was appointed to the maternal position of Chief of Training, i.e., head of the rookies. The boss figured that if I was already raising one child, what difference would a dozen more make?

80

Although I was a bit steamed at the time, looking back it was a blessing. To test my rookies' readiness for trial, I would have them practice their opening statements in front of my fidgeting infant. If they could hold Solly's attention, they were ready for trial. It was also this experience that made me realize I love to teach. Thus, when the opportunity arose a year later for me to become a full-time professor, I seized it.

No sooner did I settle into the life of a nerdy law professor than I became pregnant with my second child. Fearful of being viewed as a slacker, I somehow managed to time my delivery to coincide with winter break. I diligently finished teaching my semester's class, held tons of office hours, and headed to the hospital the day before my exam was to be administered. Of course, you know what happened next – my students called while I was in delivery! (Would they do this to a male professor? I think not.) Of course, I took the calls. What the heck. I was on morphine. They could ask anything they wanted.

My daughter was born during semester break and I was back at my post teaching five weeks later. I began that semester's class by introducing myself and stating to the students, "This is my breast. It is a food mechanism, not a sexual organ. You may be seeing it this semester. Does anyone have a problem with that?" The men were nonplussed, but there was an audible reaction by the women students. Here was their role model talking about her breast. What did this have to do with their legal education?

In truth, it had everything to do with their life education. In my twenty-three years of teaching, the question I get most from my students is not, "What are the elements of X crime?" or even, "How do I ace your exam?" The key question is inevitably, "How do you do it all? How do you balance a family life and professional life? Can I have it all?"

My answer is "yes, but it isn't easy." My second and third children were raised at the law school. I hired a research assistant (male) who was really good at changing diapers. (How's that for role reversal?!) When I became a legal commentator on high-profile cases, I had to dash between home and the courthouse for feedings and other family obligations. My kids spent their weekend "quality" time with mom at the television studios or in a sassy seat next to mom's desk. My daughter's bedtime stories were based on whatever criminal case I had taught to my students that day. Grimm's fairy tales really can't compare to stories of murder, rape, and mayhem.

Of course, I would feel guilty about this and its potential scarring effect on my child; but once again it became a blessing in disguise. My daughter, Havi, now plans to be Chief Justice of the United States. After years of sharing my professional life, she decided at age twelve that she wanted to try teaching my law school class as a guest lecturer. Usually, I invite such notables as the late Johnnie Cochran or star lawyer, Mark Geragos, to speak. One of my favorites is Janet Levine, a top woman white collar defense lawyer which is a rarity for sure. This time the students were somewhat surprised to realize that my guest speaker would be my confident (more like, "loaded for bear"), adolescent daughter. Havi and I spent days together preparing for her presentation. We pored over the law of entrapment, read the cases, talked about the law, identified policy concerns, and made a lesson plan. Some girls would prefer shopping, but they have never tried teaching criminal law.

I chose my night class for Havi's debut. When she called on the first student to recite the facts of a case and he tried to dance around the answer, Havi responded, "Surely, someone must have read the material." This mom was beaming with pride. All those years of working with her had rubbed off. It was at that moment I realized I had neither neglected my students nor my family by making the life choices I had made.

A few years later, I put an exclamation point on this revelation. In 2005, I had my first case in the United States Supreme Court. It was my great honor and pleasure to be co-counsel with the brilliant and ever so kind, Professor Erwin Chemerinsky. We represented the National Organization of Women ("NOW") in one of the abortion cases before the Court. My greatest pride was having

Havi with me. Dressed in her new Ralph Lauren suit, my daughter soaked up the experience. We entered the sanctified courtroom and Havi immediately said, "Mom, can I put a note on Chief Justice John Roberts' chair saying, 'Reserved for Havi Mirell.'" It doesn't get any better than that. Even though we lost the case 8-0 (did I mention this was an abortion case before the Roberts Court?), it was the most life-affirming moment I have had. I could be a "tough" woman litigator, law professor, role model, and mom.

I certainly don't want to give the impression that it has been easy. Even at my own institution, I have suffered indignities that men just don't have to face. For example, after fifteen years of exemplary service to the law school as a professor and Associate Dean, I was told that the next Chair to be funded would be mine. You guessed it. Funding came in for a Chair, but it wasn't given to me. Instead, the Dean selected a younger, much less senior, male colleague because he was threatening to leave and "he had a family to support." It had never occurred to me that I should be disloyal and respond to the many offers I had received to move to other institutions. I am convinced that the "guy" got the Chair because of the commonly held perception (particularly by male administrators) that a man needs the money and prestige more than his female counterparts. In their eyes, the job is a livelihood for men and a hobby for women.

No matter these obstacles, I still love being a lawyer. I didn't have any women mentors when I was starting in the profession, so I have tried extra hard to be one for my students. I regularly advise male and female students on a wide array of topics. They range from, "Professor, I think I have gotten my girlfriend in trouble, what do I do now?" to, "My professor just hit on me, what do I do now?"

Do I think it makes a difference that they have a woman to ask? Yes, I do. I answer with more experience than my male colleagues could. No, I have never hit on my students, but *every* woman I know in the legal profession was hit upon by a male teacher sometime in her educational experience. And it makes a difference that I have raised children. Children are messy, moody, and unpredictable, just like judges, students, and clients.

There are also very practical ways I have tried to help the women students in our school. My law school, in its infinite wisdom, decided that nursing moms should use the ladies' room to pump milk for their babies. That is disgusting, and I would have none of it. My office is now the semi-official lactation center for the law school. Amidst the articles, books, and cases, my women students can be women. I firmly believe that women can think deep thoughts and provide sustenance, all at the same time.

As I became one of the "senior" faculty members, I have started to ask myself whether I would have done anything differently. The simple answer is "lots." However, I wouldn't change the basics. I wouldn't give up the career, and I certainly would not give up my family. And I can prove it.

After I finished serving as the CBS Legal Commentator for the O.J. Simpson murder trial, I did some real soul searching. What was really important in my life? Although I had tried some wonderful cases, given papers across the country, served on a gaggle of Blue Ribbon Commissions, won "Professor of the Year," and sat side-by-side with Dan Rather, the best thing I have ever done was have my kids. They were the spark plugs that kept my engine running. It was for their sake, not mine, that I have remained committed to the Rule of Law.

So, I put my uterus where my mouth was and worked hard (no details on this) to have another child. The old lady did it! At an age when most professors are living off their royalties, I am attending kindergarten meetings again. And, I am doing so with mothers who are my former students. The only difference is that I am doing so in between updating my treatises.

I'm not sure what will come next, but I am sure that my experience as a lawyer has been shaped by my experience as a person. Ladies, the profession needs us. With more than 50% of the world's population being women, it is folly to believe we can

84

have a legal system dominated by men. Women see things differently, and our vision is needed in the law and elsewhere.

I once heard a saying that tends to sum it all up for me. Here it is, "I am woman. I am strong, I am exhausted!" Good luck.

Professor of Law, William M. Rains Fellow & Director, Center for Ethical Advocacy, Loyola Law School, Los Angeles. A.B., Stanford University, J.D., University of California, Los Angeles. While in law school, Laurie Levenson was chief articles editor of the UCLA Law Review. After graduation, she served as law clerk to the Honorable James Hunter III of the United States Court of Appeals for the Third Circuit. In 1981, she was appointed assistant United States Attorney, Criminal Section, in Los Angeles, where she was a trial and appellate lawyer for eight years and became the assistant division chief. She was a member of the adjunct faculty of Southwestern University Law School from 1984-1989. She joined the Loyola faculty in 1989 and served as Loyola's associate dean for academic affairs from 1996-1999. She is a legal commentator (interviewed extensively during the O.J. Simpson case), author, and most important, Proud Mother.

Mediating My Life: Confessions of a 24/7 Law Mom

Susan B. Share

One evening during our law school years, my husband and I were at a social gathering of our legal writing section when a young man, a fellow law student, joined us in conversation. He turned to Mark and said, "It's so great that your wife comes to class with you each day." An inauspicious beginning to be sure. But that was the 1980s and thankfully, we've come a long way, baby . . . or have we?

6:30 - Alarm goes off

6:40 - Wake husband

6:45 - Wake son

6:46 - Urge both son and husband to get out of bed and shower

6:47 - Prepare breakfast for Mark and Matthew; make lunches for Matthew, Rachel and Lily

7:00 - Tell Mark and Matt to come down for breakfast; it's getting cold

7:15 - Tell them to hurry up, or they'll be late

7:20 - Wake Rachel without disturbing Lily

7:30 - Mark and Matt leave; get Rachel washed, dressed, fed and ready for her carpool

7:45 - Rachel leaves

8:00 - Shower, get dressed, feed and dress Lily

8:40 - Take Lily to school

9:00 - Arrive at Lily's preschool

9:45 - Try to separate from Lily by prying her little hands from around my leg

10:15 - Back home and ready to get some legal work done

And that's if all goes well. If one of the kids is sick, forgot lunch or homework, or the laundry has piled up, or I need to go to the store, I never seem to sit down to do my "work."

Many lawyer/mothers and other female professionals make their professional lives possible by hiring nannies to take care of the children, drivers to pick the kids up from school and take them to activities, tutors to assist with their studies. I can't do that. Either because I feel it is my privilege or moral obligation or because I'm such a control freak, I need to pick up my kids from school, oversee their homework, give them dinner, maybe even chase them around the house before their bath, then read a bedtime story, and lie down with them so they fall asleep knowing they reside under a blanket of motherly love.

While that sounds fantastic, even a bit cloying, and it happens on a daily basis, our day-to-day life is laced with my own personal frustrations, outbursts, and outrage at my children's feelings of entitlement and lack of gratitude, and my own concomitant inability to find the time and energy to accomplish the tasks I set for myself each day. But I must add that Rachel will often say, "Mommy you always do so much for us; what can we do for you?" Lily will hold my face (my old, tired face) in her hands and say, "You're beautiful;" and Matthew, now much taller than me, will put his arm around my shoulder and tell me he loves me. My children keep my priorities straight.

While I admire the full-time professional woman who is able to balance her career and motherhood and of course has the requisite full-time domestic assistance either with a nanny or stay-at-home dad, that is not the choice I made. After our first child was born, I just could not leave him to go back to work; although before he was born, I really did plan to go back to work. I am completely embarrassed by this next anecdote. In fact, I hope my former boss reads this because I have wanted to apologize to her for the last fifteen years but could not bring myself to pick up the phone.

My first job after law school, even prior to receiving the bar results, was as the administrator of a mediation and arbitration program for a nonprofit organization. I loved the job and felt I would be a pioneer in alternative dispute resolution. But after six months, I was pregnant. No problem. I assured my boss, an incredible woman with four children, I would be back at work after the baby was born. In fact (this gives me the chills), I told her I planned to bring the baby to work with me, thinking the baby would sleep while I worked. Actually, I can't imagine what I was thinking. I didn't know anything about babies, but I had a quick indoctrination as soon as Matthew was born. I learned that babies don't just sleep, and I was in love. I could not stop looking at him or watching him breathe. Practically speaking, I could not afford to pay someone $10.00 an hour to stay at home with Matthew while I went to work at the nonprofit and earned perhaps $11.00 an hour. Emotionally, I just could not leave him. He was amazing, and I learned as much from him as he learned from me.

I had the privilege of staying at home with my son until he started preschool at two years, nine months. I went back to work part-time when Matthew was three. I dropped him off at school, went downtown to the office, and picked him up at 2:30. He never knew his mommy worked. I worked for a sole practitioner and gained some limited experience in probate, estate planning, and business law. While I did learn a lot, I had a major problem with the boss's secretary. She really did not want to work for a female attorney, especially one fifteen years her junior. Now that I am older, I know she would have respected me more had I been tougher. I could not win her over with kindness. In the end, I left because of her disrespect. About a month after I left, I suffered a miscarriage. The whole work situation had created a great deal of stress that I believe contributed greatly to the miscarriage. After that, I took a hiatus from law. In a year, I was happy and pregnant with Rachel.

So does motherhood and lawyering mix? I think so, but it requires a lot of sacrifices and you may have to occasionally disappoint your kids to get some work done. I work out of my house, my bedroom actually (using a post office box as my work address), which could sound erotic except that it's too multi-functional and cramped; and I don't have a cute male secretary. In fact, I am my own secretary, office administrator, rainmaker, and drone. I work at a small built-in desk next to a cupboard that houses my combination printer/fax/scanner (it also slices and dices and makes julienne fries). On the other side, the cabinets have research and client files; and those sit on top of the clothing dresser. My bedroom/office also doubles as the home gym because the treadmill stands behind me as I work. I try to minimize my overhead!

Years ago, I represented a friend in litigation involving a boundary dispute. A funny thing happened. It was the day of the depositions, and I had sent out the subpoenas. Everyone was there: the plaintiff, the defendants (my clients), defense counsel (including me and the insurance company's attorney), and the plaintiff's personal attorney. The only missing party was the attorney representing the plaintiff's insurance company. When he finally arrived, he was a huge man. He apologized for his lateness. He had gone to my office first, thinking the depositions were taking place there. What no one else in the room knew was that my "office" was a post office box about 4 x 4 x18 inches. I am still chuckling about the image of that huge man trying to fit into my mailbox.

Currently, I represent only a few clients with a variety of legal needs including small business entity formation, agreement reviews, and drafting wills and trusts. My clients are very patient, and I try

90

not to take on work that involves short deadlines. I am also doing independent contract work which includes drafting, motions, orders, notices, and subpoenas but without the stress of a partner yelling that he/she wanted it yesterday. In theory, this should create an ideal situation because I do not lose time traveling to an office, going out to lunch, schmoozing with colleagues, or kibitzing at the water cooler. The concept is that when all three of my children are in school, I can work through blocks of time and e-mail my finished work product. However, in reality, I still have to take care of the house, the laundry, the shopping, the mail, and all of the other little things that crop up on a daily basis. Therefore, it is still frustrating to find the time to devote to work. I am, however, determined to make it work; and I know that as my daughters get older, I will have more time to practice law. I feel even more strongly from personal experience that doing some intellectual work, even for just two hours a week, helps me maintain a degree of self-confidence.

I wear my self-confidence, like my heart, on my sleeve. One of my greatest difficulties is charging clients, often good friends, for the legal work I do. Almost without fail, friends and relatives have legal situations arise, and they would rather come to me than find an attorney out in the world. My time is perhaps my most valuable commodity. In the past, I have provided countless hours of legal work to friends and relatives without charging because I was so conflicted about charging the people I love. But I am no saint; in fact, they all wanted to pay and would repeatedly ask me for a bill. By not charging for the work, I felt the work I did was not worthy or was inadequate in some way. Further, I felt bad afterward that I was not contributing financially to our household. Looking back, I realize my self-esteem was at an all time low; I felt no one could value my efforts because I was not valuable. In fact, I think one reason I refuse work is because I feel too unworthy to charge for it. Now I am trying to work through this dreadful flaw and force myself to prepare bills and send them. Ultimately, my clients, whether friends or not, will respect me more.

When the children are older, I may choose to go back to work full time. I might need and enjoy the camaraderie of an office environment, or I may have the time and ambition to want to climb the partnership ladder. Or I may not. The point is that keeping my mind agile and my hand in the business is necessary so I will be ready when the time is right. Additionally, keeping abreast of changes in the law and remaining an active member of the bar also contributes to that readiness.

When I feel overwhelmed with legal work either because of the amount or the scope, I am fortunate I can always discuss the matters and issues with my attorney husband, Mark. One huge negative to having an at-home legal practice is the inability to discuss ideas with colleagues or have another attorney read over your work. I strongly believe that exchanging ideas and appropriate oversight are necessary to create the best work product. Another advantage to having a lawyer spouse is that I think only another lawyer could possibly understand some of the demands placed on an attorney by his/her job. Recently, my husband and I had invited another couple out to dinner to celebrate our friend's milestone birthday. My husband was involved in a mediation that started at nine in the morning. Reservations were for seven-thirty. At four o'clock we spoke, and Mark said he'd be through by five. We spoke again at seven, and the mediation was not finished. Mark said he would meet us at the restaurant. I called Mark after appetizers. He would be leaving soon, he thought. He showed up at nine. Fortunately, we are still friends with that couple. And of course, most fortunately, I understood.

A two lawyer marriage also poses a host of challenges. I think lawyers are inherently competitive, argumentative, controlling, and demanding. Obviously, a couple of lawyers find it easy to argue about almost anything. And the great debates flow down the line to the next generation. Our children never take no for an answer, can make a persuasive argument for bubble gum, and can argue for or against any issue whether they agree with it or not. I don't really appreciate the benefits of all of this dissension in the home; my mediation training actually serves me much better. I am constantly making peace between my two daughters and suggesting creative resolutions to the struggles over the same doll, the same book, or the last cookie.

Throughout my fifteen years of motherhood, people have, from time to time, asked me how I can just throw away my fantastic education and stay home with the kids. I have always found that question very hurtful. I don't think I am squandering my education. It's simply on hold while I devote myself to the grand effort of raising my three children to the best of my ability. I am delighted my children have the benefit of a well educated mother. From the moment they arrived, I was charged with the responsibility of teaching them everything from their alphabet to how to be moral, ethical, and caring human beings. I feel that the rescue of our society, our environment, and our future rests on our shoulders, and probably more so, on the shoulders of our children. Sending well educated, ethically responsible and prepared young people into the world may be the most important thing I do.

Reflecting on my life as a woman, a mother, a wife, and a lawyer, draws my attention to something I already know: I attempt to be all things at once, and I try to do my best at everything I do. I often fall short because it is so difficult to do so much and meet so many needs with a limited amount of time and energy. I totally downplay my lawyering in my daily life, always trying to squeeze in work between taking care of kids. Even now, when my work load has increased dramatically and all of my children are school age, I find it hard to find time to work. There are countless obligations to meet on a daily basis.

For me, being a lawyer does not define who I am. It is a great occupation, but it does not bring me my greatest fulfillment. I derive fulfillment through my children; the things they say and do on a daily basis are my sustenance. I am at a crossroads in my life. My children are growing up, and I need to re-enter the world of my peers. It's both frustrating and challenging for me because of my age coupled with my inexperience, or at least perceived inexperience. I see myself in ten or fifteen years in the role of mediator, helping people bridge their differences. For me this would be the best way I could help bring more peace into the world. I still have two young children who will require many more years of attention and direction. Our oldest is well on his way to adulthood. How I will structure the next decade of my life, I have yet to determine. Maybe it's ridiculous to even think about a plan for the future – I can barely follow a plan for tomorrow – but it's important for me to have goals, set a path to reach them, and to have hope that I can achieve them.

B.A. Reed College, J.D., Lewis & Clark College, Northwestern School of Law, both in Portland, Oregon. Susan Share lives with her husband, Mark, and their three children, Matt, Rachel, and Lily, in Sherman Oaks, California.

Moebius Strip of Work-Life Balance

Susan B. Myers

"Work-Life Balance." As a youth, hearing those words evoked an image of a blindfolded lady of justice statue, cast in bronze, and effortlessly holding her perfectly, harmonious, evenly-weighted scales. Based on that image, I believed that having work-life balance meant spending equal time, with equivalent quality of life, being at work and enjoying personal pursuits. Growing up, as I did, at the tail end of the baby-boomer, pro-feminist, "you can have it all" generation, I expected I would achieve my own work-life balance as effortlessly as the lady of justice statue. Well, here I am today, at age forty-five, looking back on where I've been and ahead to where I may be going, and I realize that the "balance" of work and life is never as simple as the evenly-weighted golden scales. Instead, my life seems less like a rigid bronze statue and more like a moebius strip. You know – that mathematical phenomenon of a one-sided continuous surface that connects to itself with a twist. A moebius strip has one outer edge and one inner edge that connect in the middle and form a figure eight (or the symbol of infinity).

The path of my life, like the moebius strip, has had more than a couple of loops and intricate twists. One key lesson I have learned is that, while it is productive and important to have a life plan and to set goals for yourself for the immediate term, at five-year intervals far into the future, life in reality is less about following a plan and more about being flexible and changing course when necessary. Starting out, I had no idea that I would end up here. "Here" for me today is at a somewhat chaotic juncture: I am juggling ten plus hour work days as a corporate attorney in private practice in a large global law firm; driving an hour each way to commute to work; single-parenting my twelve-year-old son (and vicariously experiencing all the angst he's going through as a prepubescent pre-teen); sporadically remembering to feed my cats and water the plants; trying to carve out time to visit with friends and stay in touch with far-flung family; dealing with a never-ending list of errands and house repairs; and managing my mini-household staff of nanny, housekeeper, gardener, and handyman (all of whom are essential to the smooth functioning of our household and my life). While "here" is not any place close to where I thought I would be at this point on my life plan, it seems that where I am today is where I am supposed to be. It is analogous to what my car GPS navigation system tells me each time I reach my plotted destination, no matter the location and no matter the route, "You have arrived."

Case in point: today, I am working as a corporate transactional attorney in a law firm in Los Angeles, which I joined about six months ago. Now, in my eighteenth year of practicing law, I am working in a brand new practice area, which has a very a steep learning curve, and feeling daily as if I am learning and performing at the level of a first-year associate. Prior to this job, I worked as an in-house attorney at a major corporation for eight years. I left my in-house position and re-entered private practice to join my current firm right about the time the *California Lawyer* published its winter issue cover story about the high number of women leaving private practice. Not only was I marching to a different drummer by moving back to private practice after being in-house for so many years, but

96

the firm where I now work is the same law firm that hired me straight out of law school almost nineteen years ago.

Returning to my original law firm after a fifteen-year hiatus is just one of the unexpected twists in the moebius strip that is my life. The very first loops of my moebius strip started at birth. I am the first-born child of a naval officer and a nurse, who are still married to each other after nearly fifty years! Both of my parents are highly educated and career oriented. By the time I started first grade, I had moved with my family at least five times, as we followed my dad's budding naval career. Before I started college, our family had moved at least nine times. I went to two elementary schools (in Idaho and Virginia), two high schools (in Virginia and San Diego), and two colleges (in Oregon and Washington, D.C.). My dad was on navy ships and out to sea for much of my childhood. Meanwhile, my mom, while single-handedly raising my younger brother, sister, and me, obtained her baccalaureate degree, worked full time, and went on to achieve two masters and a doctorate degree – all before her youngest child left home.

I always knew (because it was expected in my family) I would go to college and become some kind of professional. I remember I always wanted an international career, something that might replicate my dad's exotic, foreign travels. I do not remember that I always wanted to be a lawyer, but my parents will tell you otherwise. According to them, I wanted to be a lawyer and an international traveler from a very young age. The proof, they say, is evidenced by two stories they tell (to anyone who will listen, over and over again) from my early childhood. According to my mom and dad, at age two, I would traipse around our house with a large suitcase full of my favorite toys. An elderly aunt of my mom observed that someday, I was going to be a worldwide traveler. My parents' other favorite story is about my first day of kindergarten. On this momentous day, my parents drove me to school. They drove slowly through the parking lot trying to find a parking space. While they were scanning for a place to park, unbeknownst to them, I had hopped out of the slow-moving car and marched right into the school to my classroom.

When they parked and saw I was gone, they ran into the school, found my classroom, and saw me sitting at my desk with my hands folded on top. My parents say that, from that moment on, I was ready to learn and raring to go. I was on my path of becoming an attorney and having a love of international travel.

Did these early tales set my life's path? Or was my moebius strip already in place? Attending college in Washington, D.C., just a few short blocks from the White House and the State Department, I decided that the insular life of a government employee was not for me. As I finished college, I was not sure what I would do with my life. After graduation from college, retracing one path of my early life, I traveled on my own back to Asia. On that, my second trip to Asia, I lived in mainland China for six months, spent a summer working in the Philippines as an intern at the Central Bank of the Philippines, and visited Hong Kong and Taiwan. During my travels, I met with American executives from U.S. companies located in Asia and asked what skills and qualifications were important for an international focused career. The message I received from one and all was that language capability alone would not suffice – what was required was an advanced degree in a field like engineering, business, or law.

Upon returning to the States after my foreign travels, and not ready to pursue an advanced degree (certainly not in engineering or business), I got a job in Washington, D.C., at the law library of the Library of Congress in the Far Eastern law division. While working there, I decided I needed to go to law school (which is exactly what my mother had been urging me to do for several months). I studied hard for, and did well on, the LSAT, and was admitted, early admission, to Harvard Law School. During law school, I spent my first summer clerking at a Japanese law firm in Tokyo, Japan (with a side field trip to observe lawyers for a week in Seoul, Korea), and I spent my second summer at the New York, Hong Kong, and Singapore offices of a New York firm. I also took Japanese language classes through Harvard University during my second and third years of law school.

98

After taking the bar, I started my first law firm job as an attorney (at the same firm where I am working today). As a very young associate, I planned to be on the partnership fast-track. I worked long, hard hours at the firm; was sent to the firm's now former office in Tokyo, Japan, on two different occasions to work on long-term projects; and mostly gave up any kind of personal life in order to meet the firm's and my own very high expectations. While vacationing with my parents, my brother, and my then-fiancé, I was called back to work from my vacation for two back-to-back assignments. First, I left my fiancé in Sacramento with my family (whom he had met just a few days before) and flew to southern California to start my assignment. The very next day, at the completion of that project, I boarded another plane, this time en route to San Jose, the location of my second assignment. I met my fiancé in San Jose. For the next several days, I worked from early in the morning until very late each night (leaving my fiancé alone for the rest of our "vacation"). While an ordeal, I was thrilled to have been the associate chosen for these two assignments and to have been called back from vacation. That experience was very, very long ago, well before I realized the importance of having real vacation time.

As a third-year associate and a few months before my wedding, I changed law firms to continue my pursuit of an international-focused transactional practice. Not three weeks after I joined that firm, however, the sole international practice partner who had hired me left to set up his own tiny law firm. Having just switched law firms and less than ninety days from my wedding, I decided to stay at my new firm. I worked there for about seven years doing work unrelated to my international transactional career goal. The highlight of my time at that firm was going into labor while at the offices of the Attorney General. Having never been in labor before, I did not realize that the twinges and discomfort I felt during settlement discussions actually signaled the start of my labor. I completed the negotiations, went back to the office, worked until late in the evening, and drove home. Instead of going to work the next day, however, I ended up going to the hospital that night and having my son the next day.

Once my son was born, my focus and drive totally shifted. Suddenly the "brass ring" of partnership at a big law firm no longer seemed important. I wanted more time to devote to my family and thought I could better serve this purpose by finding an in-house position. So, I left my second firm and joined the legal department of a Japanese automobile finance services company. While the in-house job was somewhat more manageable than being an associate in a law firm, I still spent quite a bit of time traveling for business, going to Japan, Brazil, Puerto Rico, Argentina, Venezuela, and Mexico City. I also took an assignment for a two-year tour in Nagoya, Japan, moving there with my family in August 2000. Soon after getting settled, my marriage disintegrated. Being without sufficient resources in a foreign county, I could not find a way to continue my assignment while taking care of my son and going through my divorce. So, with the help of my company, I ended my assignment early and returned to the States to live with my parents in Utah.

I managed to retain my in-house position through the ordeal of my divorce and decided to live with my son at my parents' house in Utah for the next six years. During that time, I commuted to Los Angeles on a weekly, part-time basis. Despite the difficulties of a weekly state-to-state commute, there was no way I was going to take another bar exam so I could work in Utah. Having my parents to care for my son while I was in Los Angeles alleviated some of my guilt about being away from home so much. However, returning to live with my parents at age forty, with young son (and our two cats) in tow, presented its own set of issues and stresses that had never been plotted on the plan for my life.

After completing my five-year stint of alimony obligations (yes, I had to pay him even though I have sole custody of our child), and when my son was entering seventh grade, I decided to move back to California. Last summer, while searching for housing close to my office, a partner from my old law firm contacted me. I thought he wanted to get together for lunch, as we did from time to time periodically during my tenure in-house. When I told him I was moving back to Los Angeles at the end of the summer, he offered me a job in the position of counsel in their finance practice. So, after moving my child, my two cats, and our two cars of stuff from Utah to California, setting up my new household, and enrolling my son in his new school (all of which had been in the then-current plan), I detoured from my most recent career path and started my next adventure – on yet another new twist along the path of my moebius strip.

This limerick sums it all up for me:

A mathematician confided
That a Moebius band is one-sided,
And you'll get quite a laugh,
If you cut one in half,
For it stays in one piece when divided.

B.A., Phi Beta Kappa, The George Washington University, J.D., Harvard Law School. Susan Myers was the articles editor/associate editor, Harvard International Law Journal. She is Counsel at Mayer, Brown, Rowe & Maw, LLP. Her current practice areas are banking and finance, equipment leasing, and international transactions. She started her legal career at Mayer, Brown in 1988, moved to McKenna & Cuneo, LLP, then worked in-house for Toyota Motor Credit Corporation. She attended Beijing Foreign Languages Institute. She has a working knowledge (reading, writing, speaking) of Japanese and Mandarin Chinese.

My Life-long Commitment to Equal Justice and Civil Rights

Barbara J. Cox

It was 1969 when, at age thirteen, I decided to become a lawyer. The turbulence of those times had even reached my home town of Lexington, Kentucky. I marched in anti-war and civil rights marches and fought with my father about the Vietnam War and the Kent State shootings two years later. But it was reading Karl Menninger's book, *The Crime of Punishment*, that made me decide to pursue a legal career.

Now, thirty-seven years later, I have little memory about the book's specifics. Menninger wrote about the terrible conditions in U.S. prisons and the denial of civil rights to inmates. What I do remember is how shocked I was that a supposedly civilized society would treat its criminals in such a horrid fashion. Of course, I was as naive and idealistic as most teens; and I had no basis to understand the viewpoint from those mandated to house some of the country's most difficult men and women. But the book sparked in me a need to try to help right those injustices, a need that has not left me.

Interestingly, the problems that almost kept me from pursuing this dream began at about the same time. I started using alcohol and drugs at thirteen, and my abuse increased steadily over the next ten years. I managed to earn good grades throughout this time, perhaps convincing myself that my use was not a problem since I was able to continue to earn As in high school and college. I even managed to do well on the LSAT and was admitted to the University of Wisconsin Law School despite using drugs on a daily basis for over seven years. Like many of my peers during the 1970s, we would sit in bars or in crummy apartments, ranting against the establishment and punctuating our distrust of it with our refusal to heed the nation's drug laws.

Despite my descent into drug addiction and alcoholism, I kept alive that part of me that wanted to help those who were imprisoned. As a senior at Michigan State, I did a full semester internship with the Michigan Department of Corrections. This included visits to some of the state's prisons, including the infamous Jackson Prison. Going inside the massive, four-story building and walking the locked wards was shocking for me. I walked through one cell block, open in the middle and surrounded with four levels of men in cells. I walked by prisoners in cells on the first floor, and the prison officials cared little that a young woman was walking by men who were half-undressed or using the toilet in clear sight. I understood then that one of the most significant rights taken from prisoners is their right to privacy – their right to private space in which to live their lives. To me, that loss seemed almost more overwhelming than the brutality they faced in prison and their loss of freedom.

I continued my interest in helping inmates as a law student. Following my first year, I worked for the Legal Assistance to Inmates Program, a clinical program at the law school. With three other women, we drove weekly to the women's prison in Fond du Lac, Wisconsin, to meet with our clients. Our work was not related to

104

their convictions or appeals, but instead our mandate was to help prisoners access those rights granted them by the prison system. We helped document jail time already served so it could be applied against the women's sentences, helped them with civil law matters such as child custody and access to state benefits for the families they had left behind, and tried to ensure they had access to as many educational or training options available to them. I was repeatedly struck by the shiver that went through my system every time I walked into the prison and heard the gates slam behind me. Even knowing that my "incarceration" was only for a few hours and that I had the ability to leave when I chose, the slam of the gates scared me in a way that little else did. I could not imagine the horror these women felt when the gates slammed behind them, knowing it would be years before they could escape their confinement.

After eight months working with LAIP and eight months working for one of the program's directors helping to write administrative regulations for the Wisconsin Department of Corrections, I left the criminal justice field for good. It wasn't that I was disillusioned, but I had encountered a new injustice that demanded my attention even more.

Five years earlier, I had come out as a lesbian after falling in love with a college friend who I met while taking the same classes, living in the same dorm, and studying together. While working in the dormitory kitchen one day, I almost dropped a full pan of hot food when it suddenly became clear to me that I was in love with my friend. I dismissed the feeling almost immediately, knowing in 1976 that women did not fall in love with their women friends. It was not until a few months later when we both got up the nerve to act on our feelings that I realized that such a love was possible. We hid our relationship for the next two years, staying in the dorms and living as suite-mates.

I had gotten clean and sober in November of my first semester of law school, after months of going to school high or hung-over from partying the night before. Somehow, perhaps simply because of the shock to my system from being clean and sober after years of abuse, I managed to earn excellent grades that first year and was invited to join the law review. I maintained those grades throughout law school despite struggling to free myself from the compulsion to drink and to use drugs. At times, I am sure that having to focus in such a concentrated way on my studies helped me to maintain a clean and sober lifestyle, one that has continued for more than twenty-seven years.

But I became politicized about the legal discrimination facing lesbians and gay men after I was asked to join the law review. One of the topics the editorial board suggested to its new recruits was to write about the Miriam ben Shalom case recently decided by the Wisconsin Eastern District federal court. Contrary to the few previously decided cases, the judge in that case found that the military had violated Ms. ben Shalom's rights after dismissing her simply for acknowledging she was a lesbian. Although the case was ultimately reversed on appeal to the Seventh Circuit, I did my research and writing while the case was making history as one of the first to protect lesbians from legal discrimination. I now understood that my work to help end injustice would focus on pursing rights for lesbians, gay men, bisexuals, and transgendered (LGBT) people.

After finishing law school and clerking for Judge Dykman on the Wisconsin Court of Appeals, I made another discovery that would change the path of my career. Although I had flirted with the idea of getting a Ph.D. in history and becoming a professor while in college, I now had the opportunity to teach at the University of Wisconsin Law School. Hired on a two-year, limited term basis to help run the school's legal writing program, I kept that job for four years and combined it with a joint appointment in the Women's Studies Program. Teaching legal writing to law students and Women and the Law to women's studies majors made me realize that teaching would be my career. I have never lost the passion that was awakened in me with that first teaching position.

In 1987, I left Wisconsin for California Western School of Law in San Diego, seeking a tenure-track position that would also allow me to teach substantive courses. After running the legal writing program for several years, I moved completely into teaching substantive courses and earned tenure in 1991.

Today, I am one of those people who kisses her name plate on the office door when I arrive each morning. I love teaching, being able to work with students, discovering the intricacies of the legal system and how to use the system to help clients. I teach mainly first-year courses: Civil Procedure I and II, and Property II, as well as seminars in Women and the Law, Sexual Orientation and the Law, and Comparative Family, Gender, and Sexuality.

I have been fortunate to have a career that also allows me to do equal justice work. The idea that I am paid to write in areas that are important to me still amazes me. My early writings were in advanced legal writing, domestic partnership, and abortion rights. Since 1983 when I was president of the Madison, Wisconsin, Equal Opportunities Commission and co-chaired its Alternative Families' Taskforce, I have focused my attention on obtaining legal rights and recognition for LGBT couples. In 1983, Madison was one of only a handful of municipalities, including San Francisco and West Hollywood, considering ordinances to protect same-sex couples. We were literally making up the concepts as we worked on the issues, talking with employers, insurance agencies, church and civil rights leaders, and couples.

Twenty-three years later, I am proud to have been engaged on the ground floor of a movement that has obtained marital rights in several countries, nationwide registration in countless others, and judicial protections around the country. We have marriage in Massachusetts; civil unions in Vermont, Connecticut, New Jersey, and New Hampshire; domestic partnerships in California and Oregon; and more limited partnership recognition in Hawaii, Maine, Washington, and the District of Columbia. Despite suffering through countless constitutional battles where citizens from more than half the states have written discrimination into their state constitutions banning same-sex couples from the simple protections offered to all other couples who can marry, we finally won our first statewide battle in Arizona in November 2006. Preventing a discriminatory constitutional amendment has energized a movement weary from so many electoral defeats.

I now serve as co-chair of the executive and steering committees of Freedom to Marry, the only national organization whose sole focus is to win marriage equality for same-sex couples. We have won several cases recognizing that depriving same-sex couples of marital status violates the state constitutions of many states. And we have won our first legislative campaigns in California and Connecticut and our first electoral battle in Arizona. Even though it seems the movement is proceeding at a glacial pace, I have seen the progress from those early days in 1983 when we did not even dare hope that marriage might some day be possible. My scholarship focuses on interstate recognition of the marriages and domestic partnerships or civil unions of same-sex couples, and I regularly speak around the country on these issues.

My work on marriage finds some ties with the early struggles I pursued to obtain rights for prisoners. More than twenty years ago, the U.S. Supreme Court recognized that prisoners have a fundamental right to marry, even while in prison and despite separation for years from their chosen spouses. One day, I am sure that the Supreme Court will also find that same-sex couples also have a fundamental right to marry.

My legal career has taken many twists from that first day in 1969 when I knew I wanted to be a lawyer. But the passion that was born at that time continues to this day, as I try to help obtain and protect the rights of those facing discrimination. Although I could not have imagined, at age thirteen, what my career would hold, I am proud to see the results of those early dreams. Law has been a fabulous career for me, and I am grateful every day that I had the opportunity to pursue this dream.

B.A., Michigan State, J.D., University of Wisconsin. Barbara Cox is Professor of Law at California Western School of Law. She has been married to Peg Habetler since 1992 (private commitment ceremony) and since 2003 (legal marriage in Canada). She wrote Beyond the Basics: A Text for Advanced Legal Writing (2d ed. 2003) (with Mary Barnard Ray). She has written two book chapters and sixteen law review articles on obtaining and protecting legal recognition for same-sex couples. In addition, she has written numerous other articles in the areas of abortion rights, sexual orientation discrimination, and racial discrimination. She served as associate dean for academic affairs at California Western and as deputy director for the Association of American Law Schools. She has chaired the AALS sections on women and on sexual identity.

New Choices

Helen I. Zeldes

I recently joined the stay-at-home mommy club. More precisely, the work-from-home mommy club. The presumptive death knell for my career. A statistic in the headcount of women hemorrhaging from law firms. No longer would I be part of a power machine, a firm so powerful that politicians took our calls personally. No longer would I have an army of people to work with – just my little desk in my spare room, cat on bed, child in the other room. Going from suing large corporations, up against the largest defense firms in the country, working on mega multi-million dollar cutting edge cases, making mega bucks, and having teams of people behind (and in front) of me . . . to working alone in my office/guest room, library in closet, answering my own office line. No secretary, no paralegal, no document clerk, no fax clerk, no mail room. No partners over me. No paycheck. I was alone, but I was free! I no longer needed to plead for time with my daughter, with my family. And you know, strange things have happened. Cases are flooding in. Big firms want to finance them. Banks are throwing money at me. I am taken seriously. I'm more successful and respected than ever. Not exactly what I thought the first year "at home" would be like, but the field of law is not exactly what I thought it would be. Of course, I was a bit naive going into it.

Prior to law school, I spent most of my adult life working for myself. All of my businesses were owned and run by women. When I saw talent, I promoted, empowered, and encouraged women. I created flexible work environments that nurtured my employees' lives. Many of my employees had children along the way. The manager of my gallery brought her baby to work with her when she was ready to come back from maternity leave. She set up a play area and worked alongside her daughter. It took her a while to get back into full swing as the manager, and the business suffered a bit; but all these years later (her daughter is now nine years old), she has stuck with me. For fourteen years, she has watched my back while I wandered off to law school and then moved out of state to pursue my new career. I invested in her, made sacrifices for her, and she did the same for me. The women's way, the women's club.

Entering the field of law (the ultimate old boy's club) was a definite shock. One of the first things I noticed was that I was frequently the only woman lawyer in the room, whether it was a deposition, a hearing, or at trial. There were other women of course: court reporters, secretaries, paralegals, but not many lawyers. Why, if women were going to law school in equal numbers as men, was I surrounded by pants? As I would later find out, the attrition rate for women leaving the career quickly and vastly surpasses men. Statistically, most women have children at some point in their lives and are faced with a turning point in their careers. With the traditional law job requiring fifty to sixty or more hours a week and part-time relegating women to mommy track, or worse – demotion to lesser office space, no part-time option at all – women who choose to have children have had to choose between marginalization and departure.

When I had my first child, that painful choice became mine. For the first time in my life, I faced the glass ceiling and the mommy wall. I knew I had to make a decision: relegation to mommy track, leave my baby with other caretakers for ten to twelve or more hours a day, or leave my job. After much soul searching, I knew I could not walk down the mommy track, being punished because I had a

112

child. I could not continue working sixty hour weeks, frequently not getting home in time to say goodnight to my baby, feeling horrible when I dropped her off early in the morning at day care and in all likelihood still feel like I was on mommy track because of the perception I was not as available as I once was. So, what real choice was there?

Although the idea of starting my own practice was scary – my entire legal career had been spent working with teams of people – working for myself was familiar ground. Starting my own stay-at-home mom law practice is actually my eighth business. I went into business just barely out of college, at age twenty-two, with a Guatemalan imports and jewelry booth at the Aloha Stadium Flea Market in Hawaii. I did not have any experience or financing to speak of. What I did have was a good idea and $500 credit available on a credit card. I ordered just what product I needed to get through the next week, building the business until a great retail location became available (my second business). I went on to open a café (my third), an eco-shop (fourth), a line of clothing I designed and manufactured (fifth), and then the business that outlasted them all, my gallery (sixth), still alive and well on the North Shore of Oahu. After taking many years off to pursue my career in law, I'm now re-emerging as the hands-on CEO of my gallery and launching my first online store (seventh). Starting my own non-traditional law practice (eighth) is in many ways coming full circle. At each juncture, I weighed the risks, and the risk of failure has been acceptable to me. Worse has always been the risk of never trying and never knowing what could have been.

You need not have an M.B.A. (I don't) or business experience (I didn't) to go out on your own; in fact, I have helped many women start businesses who had no business experience at all. Women must start their own law businesses because women do things differently than men, in law and in business. A recent study showed that 83% of law firm partners are still men! We will not achieve parity in partnerships in law firms until somewhere around 2088. Mothers make less money than our childless counterparts, but we all

113

still make less than men. (I recently read that women without children earn 90% of men's salaries, while mothers earn a mere 60%.) Since we lack an old boy's network, an old boy's club (we don't exactly fit in there anyway), we must make an affirmative and conscious commitment to help each other, support each other's businesses, encourage each other. We can make equity a reality for ourselves, in our lifetimes, but we must leap out and create a new field of law that supports, respects, and honors us – that thrusts us up our own ladders. Why? Not because the field of law needs us as some argue (though it does), but because we choose the field of law. We have every right to a high paying career of our choice, not to be treated punitively because we are women, not to be punished for being the child bearers (and still for most, the primary caretakers) of our species.

I answer my office phone in my pajamas once in a while. I can be on conference calls at 6:00 a.m. with my co-counsel from New York and still spend time with my daughter before the babysitter arrives. I change diapers mid-day. I take my daughter to the park in the afternoon. Sometimes I spend an entire "workday" with her. I love motherhood and not having to choose between her and success. And I still go toe-to-toe with the biggest law firms and against the largest corporations in the country. I fight harder now; I play a leaner game; every minute counts, and I cannot afford to lose. I have not been penalized for leaving the mainstream. Indeed, I am happier and more successful than ever. I will hire other moms (and dads). I hope you will, too. Come join me, take the leap. Forge a new future. You're not alone.

B.A., University of California, Davis, J.D., University of Hawaii, William S. Richardson School of Law, cum laude. During law school, Helen Zeldes served as a member and editor of law review and following graduation clerked for the Honorable Daniel R. Foley at the Intermediate Court of Appeals for the State of Hawaii. She is licensed to practice law in Hawaii and California. Helen served on the Board of Directors of Hawaii Women Lawyers, on the Board of San Diego CoastKeeper and San Diego Girls Alliance. She is currently being recruited by new boards and is trying not to over-commit herself, though she feels deeply drawn to the fight to stop global warming. Before starting her own practice, Helen practiced law at the San Diego office of Lerach Coughlin (formerly Milberg Weiss) from 2000-2006. Helen's practice areas include complex class action litigation focusing on consumer and insurance fraud, human rights, civil rights, employment, and environmental law.

Once a Mentor, Always a Mentor

Samantha S. Goodman

I find it amazing that I have practiced law in a big firm for almost ten years. I was one of those people who graduated from law school thinking I would work in a big firm for two or three years until something better and more flexible came along – a job in law that would allow me to both work and raise a family. And why have I stayed in big firm practice? Because I was lucky enough to find amazing mentors, flexible employers, and a satisfying and fulfilling profession.

I remember being a summer associate like it was yesterday. All summer associates were required to rotate through at least three departments during the summer. My first rotation was in real estate, and my first assignment was for the man who made me the lawyer I am today. I remember sitting in his office my first day. What an office! To say Michael is a sports enthusiast is an understatement. His office was (and still is) filled floor to ceiling with sports memorabilia and awards. Even the windows are covered. I was terrified sitting in Michael's office that day since I was sitting in the office of arguably one of the finest and most well known real estate lawyers in the country. I remember him telling me I had the personality of a real estate lawyer. To this day, I do not know how he knew this to be true. I knew after my summer that I wanted to be a real estate lawyer and was thrilled to be offered the job. I started the next fall in the real estate group working directly for Michael and his partners, John and Jackie. It did not take long before I realized I was working with a special group of people.

I worked very hard my first year; and I must admit, I did not enjoy it. I worked late nights, weekends, and holidays. I never enjoyed a three-day weekend during my entire first year practicing law. This was demonstrating your commitment to Michael. You had to prove to him you were willing to do what he asked, meet his deadlines, and work hard. Once you proved yourself, it became easier.

Michael is a big believer in family. Thankfully, he more than approved of my choice of a spouse. In fact, he likes to take credit for my choice (and I have had to remind him on numerous occasions that I had found Andrew before I was a summer associate). I mention this because once I proved myself during my first year of practice, Michael made a point of making sure I spent time with my then boyfriend, then fiancé, and finally husband.

Michael liked Andrew so much that he became involved in planning my engagement. He was responsible for driving me to the Peninsula Hotel for a "client" meeting where he watched Andrew propose to me. He was also involved in my wedding. He actually wanted to walk me down the aisle with my dad; however, I informed him this was a job reserved for my parents. Instead, we gave him the title of "Managing Father" (he was the firm's managing partner at the time), and he carried the rings down the aisle and supervised the flower girls. I remember as I started to walk down the aisle with my parents, my dad started to cry, which caused me and my mom to cry. Michael, who walking in front of us, turned around and said, "Why are you crying? I'm the one who won't have Sam available for two weeks while she's on her honeymoon!" We all laughed. He also gave the nicest and most heartfelt speech at my wedding. One of

118

my husband's friends came up to me after the speech and asked if it was really genuine – it was. I already knew how fortunate I was, but I knew it even more after my wedding.

I had found a mentor who believed in working hard but who also believed in the work-life balance. This is not to say that working in a big firm environment did not take its toll. I was consistently working twelve plus hour days and working most weekends. So when I received a job offer to become in-house counsel the year after I was married, I jumped at the chance to leave big firm practice. It sounded like the perfect job. No billable hour requirement. No working weekends or late nights. I agonized over my decision to leave. Michael was more than just a boss. He and the entire real estate group, especially Michael, John and Jackie, had become my extended family. Giving notice was one of the hardest things I have ever had to do. I owed Michael, John, and Jackie so much; however, I felt I saw too little of my husband, experienced too much stress, and could not imagine how I could ever work that hard and have kids. Michael asked me to stay and consider becoming a part-time attorney. I told him it was an amazing offer, but I did not want to be perceived as lazy. I had a fundamental problem with being an associate who was not required to work as hard as the partners. Michael gave me a great send off and told me I could always come back.

I was back after a month and a half. The new job was not the perfect job for many reasons – one of the biggest reasons was that I missed the family atmosphere and congenial environment I had left behind. So I returned to big firm life and accepted Michael's offer to become a part-time attorney. I was the first female attorney to become part-time without children. What Michael realized was that it was better to allow me to reduce my schedule to alleviate some of the stress of the big firm billable requirement than to allow years of training to walk out the door. Thankfully, the firm agreed.

A few years later, I had my first child. Michael was so excited for me and Andrew and so supportive. He wanted to make sure I would return to work after maternity leave. I remember having long talks with my husband while I was on maternity leave about being a working mom. Andrew felt it was important for our daughter to have a working mom role model (and he liked my pay check, too). I agonized over my decision to return to work; but having had a working mom as well, I knew my daughter would not suffer. In fact, I felt she would benefit in many ways. I remember telling my husband that if I were not working for such an understanding and supportive boss and for a firm that supported my part-time schedule, I probably would not return. I did return and reduced my schedule to four days a week. Again, Michael supported my decision; and I started the next phase of my legal career – as a working mom.

Soon after returning from maternity leave, most of my group left to join a new firm. I was excited about the new opportunity until I realized the new firm was not the place for me. The firm seemed only to value its partners. I found myself, for the first time, feeling I had to make partner. This was a new goal for me. Success means different things to different people. For me, success in life does not mean being a partner. It means being a committed lawyer who does excellent work for her clients as well as being a great wife and mother. At my new firm, however, I felt that unless I was a partner, I was dispensable; and I did not want to be in a position where I was leaving my kids every day to work for a firm that did not value me. I soon learned that my quest for partnership was going to be a problem. The person in charge of reviewing all associates nationwide was a man in his sixties. The first thing he said to me when I sat down for my first review was, "So how many years have you been part-time?" It did not seem to matter to him that my reviews were excellent and that I had brought in a significant amount of business. While the firm presented itself as part-time friendly, I realized during my review that was not the case. For the second time in my legal career, I found myself agonizing over my decision to leave the firm and my outstanding mentors.

I was presented with an opportunity to join another firm as Counsel based on an existing client relationship. The firm hired me part-time. As it turns out, the firm also hired me pregnant. My new firm is part-time friendly and seems to value my work product and client relationships more than billable hours. The best part is that I left on extremely good terms with Michael, John, and Jackie, and I speak to them often. I still call them when I have questions, and they are all available and happy to advise me.

I do not think you will find any working mother who will tell you it is easy. I still feel guilty as I leave for work. It actually gets harder as children get older and can communicate their feelings. When my older daughter looks me in the eye as I am leaving for work and says, "Mommy, please don't go," it breaks my heart. But, I honestly feel I am doing the right thing for my children and for myself. In a perfect world, I would probably have left law until my children started school; however, law, in general, and real estate, specifically, is about relationships and knowledge. I know if I quit working for a few years, it would be hard to return at the same level.

Part of deciding to be a part-time lawyer is realizing that the work may not get done as quickly as it used to; and it may not be absolutely perfect, but that is okay. It is not about accepting mediocrity but about accepting your limits and managing client expectations. Most of all, it is about never apologizing for being part-time. My clients know I have children and support my decision to balance work and life. My feeling is that there are thousands of lawyers in the world; and if a client does not value my decision to prioritize my children, that client can find another lawyer.

I feel very fortunate. I have an amazing family, including an extremely encouraging, accommodating, and helpful husband. I have a good job. I certainly could not have done it all without my family and my wonderful, supportive mentors. The nice part is that even though I joined a new firm, my mentors are still my mentors. In fact, I recently worked on a transaction with Michael. It was very interesting working on a deal on the opposite side of my former boss. It was really important for me to impress him with what he had taught me over the years. During a phone conversation discussing various issues, he asked me to modify a provision in the lease document. I listened intently while taking notes; and while I was taking notes, he lowered his voice and said, "You know you should say no, right?" Once a mentor, always a mentor!

B.A., University of California, Los Angeles, J.D., Loyola Law School, Los Angeles. Samantha Goodman joined Bryan Cave LLP as Counsel in 2005 as a member of the real estate client service group. She concentrates her practice in real estate leasing. She is a frequent lecturer on landlord and tenant law in California. Samantha has been named a "Southern California Rising Star" for 2004, 2005, 2006 and 2007 in a poll among Southern California Super Lawyers conducted by Law and Politics and Los Angeles magazines. In addition, she was named one of "The Southland's Rising Young Stars Under 40" by Real Estate Southern California in 2005. Most recently, Samantha received the Los Angeles County Bar Association Real Property Section "outstanding young lawyer award." Prior to joining Bryan Cave LLP, Samantha was a Senior Associate at Pillsbury Winthrop Shaw Pittman LLP and DLA Piper US LLP. She is the proud mother of Sydney and Allyson.

Raising Happy, Productive Children on a Workingwoman's Schedule

Julie P. Dubick

It's startling to have worked for thirty-five years. I don't feel old; what I do feel is how fast it's gone. Of course, I didn't believe time would fly when I was struggling to manage work and family – I only felt I wasn't giving either enough. With historical perspective, I have learned some of what works and what doesn't. Having traversed the working terrain from public service to private practice, associate to rainmaking partner in a corner office, golden handcuffs to no salary, law practice to a new career, all the while raising three children and maintaining a marriage, a hard working but not exceptional woman can compete successfully in a demanding career and still manage to raise happy, productive children.

I had expected that the influx of women would substantially change the legal profession, but the more it changed, the more it stayed the same. When I started law school, women were less than 10% of the class. Today, women make up 50% or more of the class, yet the number of women partners remains as small as when I started. When I first interviewed in law firms, men asked about my plans for children and wondered out loud about training women who'd likely leave when they got pregnant. Today, no one asks about family plans; and many law firms have instituted part-time work, often referred to as the "mommy track." Yet women continue to either postpone childbearing to make partner or complain that the "mommy track" relegates them to meaningless work with no hope of partnership. When I started private practice, quality of life was not an issue; associates were eager to work grueling hours for the privilege of partnership. Today, balancing work and family is discussed and debated; yet, hourly minimum requirements continue to rise along with the number of years it takes to make partner. These requirements are almost impossible for any associate to legitimately complete, but they take a particular toll on women trying to juggle work and children. Balancing these demands was hard when I started thirty-five years ago and has not improved.

I graduated law school in 1974 and headed to the United States Department of Justice where hiring opportunities for women, especially litigators, were greater than in private practice. I wasn't worried about work-family balance; I was solely interested in pursuing my career without interruptions. Women were establishing their independence and earning power; in fact, I had to explain why I took my husband's last name without at least hyphenating it. The Justice Department offered a wonderful opportunity for young lawyers to learn on the job. There were no senior partners, junior partners, or senior associates to hog the cases that went to trial, and the number of trials far exceeded the number of lawyers. Everyone listened, even to a young lawyer, who stood up in court and announced, "I represent the United States of America and here is our position." Working at the Justice Department made me feel I was contributing to national issues and improving lives. When the opportunity to stay at the Justice Department in a higher paying, more substantial job was offered, I happily accepted.

As I was moving to the Department's United States Marshals Service, as General Counsel and Associate Director, I became pregnant; and at the then ripe old age of twenty-nine, I gave birth to our first child. To my surprise, I fell immediately and completely in love. Even though this was a time when women competed to see who could return faster to work after childbirth – a federal judge announced from the bench she had only taken three days off – I took the full six weeks of maternity leave. The first year of baby and work was a blur; but for me, working kept me eager to come home to my child and the government job permitted me to do so at reasonable hours.

At the Marshals Service, I learned to shoot a weapon, deal with law enforcement issues, and supervise a staff of lawyers and then approximately 300 people as Assistant Director. It was interesting work that dealt with unusual issues like the right to hide children of divorced parents in the Witness Protection Program and overcrowding of federal prisons. Had I understood how good I had it, I would have resisted leaving when the Administration changed. But the call to private practice, constantly reinforced in law school, was strong. My husband was ready for a change, and his job opportunities took us to California with the opportunity to enter private practice. By the early 80s, law firms were seriously exploring hiring women for associate positions outside the wills and trusts departments. I had trial experience – a rare condition for a young lawyer. So, even though lateral transfers were then frowned upon, I had a choice of several firms and chose the only firm in San Diego that actually had a woman partner. She was a divorce attorney with an outstanding reputation who was about ten years older than I. When she graduated at the top of her class from Columbia Law School, she was unable to find a legal job; so she postponed her career until she had put her husband through medical school and had her twins enrolled in kindergarten. Then she put out her shingle;

125

shortly thereafter, she had a matter opposite the firm's senior partner who offered her a job when she won the case. She was totally supportive of other women, something that unfortunately turned out not to be commonly true, and was a great role model. For me, this was a turning point. I'd not had a female role model. There were few female supervisors at the Justice Department and none at the Marshals Service. My mother had married at twenty-one and literally sent me off to college to find a husband, as her mother had done for her. This was challenging because I had chosen a girls' college and started college with strictly enforced curfews, and men were not allowed off the dorm's first floor. By my junior year, I switched to a newly coed men's college where men and women shared the same bathroom. My mom was sincerely disappointed I was not engaged by senior year, and my younger sister getting engaged and married before me didn't help. Mom was always supportive, but having a senior female partner who had raised great kids was inspiring.

Turns out I needed the inspiration because for me, private practice was shocking. I had gone from first chair and largely in control of my schedule to an associate. Granted I was working for the head of litigation, a lawyer with outstanding legal skills who unfortunately needed to be convinced that my government service had taught me a great deal. He had risen to the top by tightly controlling his cases, including anyone who worked on them. My first year, I only half joked that on my way to work my car would automatically veer into the mental health building located two blocks from the law firm. I don't remember asking my not yet two-year-old daughter her opinion of mommy's changed lifestyle, but I do remember the constant worry about work when I was home and home when I was at work. I could have taken a hint when my daughter's earliest words were "Mommy book" while I studied for the California bar and "Mommy meeting" after I started working. Within the year, she was talking in full sentences with a lovely Caribbean lilt. At first I didn't understand why people asked me about her accent until I realized she spoke like our Caribbean

126

housekeeper with whom she was spending more time than with me. If I had to work the full number of years to partnership, I would have been long gone. The hours were too long, sitting second chair too frustrating, and the time away from my daughter too unacceptable.

Two years after I joined the firm and six months pregnant, I made partner. Partnership meant a significant salary/benefit package and keys to a car leased by the firm. It did not mean membership in the old boy's club, even within the firm. Partnership is an accomplishment; but once I made it, the work feeding tube was removed and I was expected to generate my own work. My partnership ride began with one child in kindergarten and one in diapers. I had full time help and a supportive husband, and yet felt I didn't have enough time for either my work or my children. I was always late – except for court – and always felt like I needed to apologize for something. I missed school plays, athletic events, dinners, bath times, and even a birthday and felt guilty about every one of them and more.

I made plenty of mistakes, but the press of time did require a focused approach. Not being readily available forced my children to make their own choices, which taught them not to be afraid of decisions. I often asked them for their opinions and followed them, which contributed to a sense of confidence in their abilities. I needed to set high standards for their schoolwork, behavior, and attitude toward others; and I didn't have time to waiver. Since I wasn't there to bend these rules, they more often than not had to push themselves to meet the expectations they'd been given. This helped them learn to try harder and gave them a sense of accomplishment when they succeeded. And, most important, I was fiercely loyal. They knew they were my highest priority because I told them every day. They knew I would speak up for them and fight for them if they needed help. Once I became a school's worst nightmare when my son was wrongly excluded from a program he had qualified for, and I helped my daughter sell the most Girl Scout cookies when she decided that was important. For me, not seeing them until dinnertime helped me be more consistent in my responses to their behavior and more tolerant of their foibles.

My kids grew up, my law practice marched on, and my name moved up the letterhead. I became the first female partner named to the executive committee and developed enough business to make me and the associates assigned to me highly profitable. I won cases and lost some but was always diligent and devoted to my clients. On a personal level, I thoroughly enjoyed supervising and mentoring associates and took pride in their advancement. I organized the women associates and partners in training programs, holidays, and business development activities. On a firm level, I tried and failed to move the firm forward in ways I believed better accommodated women and minorities including making decision-making more transparent, committing to diversity hiring, using more objective criteria for salary allocation, and permitting a quality part-time track. My failure to effect changes at the firm seemed to echo the failure of women in general to improve conditions for working mothers. For example, when I started working in the 1970s, there were few available childcare options; more than a quarter century later with a huge increase in the number of working women, there are still few good childcare options.

Just as my two older children were becoming independent and my practice was flourishing, I became pregnant again. An embarrassed fourteen-year-old and surprised ten-year-old discovered they were going to have a sister. She turned out to be a source of joy for all of us and the glue that kept her older sister and brother attached to the family as they moved from high school to college. But starting all over after almost twenty years of juggling work and family was the beginning of the end. I began to evaluate my practice. For me, too much of it was spent defending large companies. Winning meant moving pots of money from one large entity to another. At the same time, my son was growing quickly and almost ready to graduate high school, and now I had been given one more chance to raise a child. I knew it was time to leave. I wanted to spend my time differently, but I was afraid to give up my identity as a partner in a large firm and to give up my income. I spent five years discussing quitting and probably drove my husband crazy, and it finally took a risky decision to run for school board to get me to take a one-year leave of absence. I lost a bruising election, turned fifty with twenty-five years of law practice, and my mother died in her 70s, reminding me in the hardest way that life is too short. I gave up the corner office, my retirement fund, and resigned.

The transition from full time practice to stay-at-home mom wasn't easy. It took a long time for me to adjust. The loss of my salary was my own major stumbling block, and it caused me to question my contribution to the family. I understood for the first time the pressure on women who don't work outside the home and the discomfort of having to ask for money. My son was initially terrified his mother was home and could turn her full attention to him. My six-year-old was delighted; I'd be there to pick her up from school. I was shocked – yet amused – the first time I proudly showed up right after school let out (instead of at 6:00 p.m.) to have my daughter announce, "Mommy, you're too early; I want to play longer. Can you come back later?" All those working years worrying that my children were the lonely, last children to be picked up from school had been for naught. On the bright side, I had the time to exercise and gave in to adopting the dog my daughter desperately wanted. I was able to attend all of my son's senior year football games and plan my older daughter's wedding, ironically while she finished her final year of law school and studied for the bar. My daughter is now happily married and in private practice in Los Angeles, and my son just graduated from Yale and is working in his dream job in Washington, D.C. The youngest is in seventh grade and happily involved in school, sports, and friends.

As for me, while I was figuring out my new identity, I was lucky enough to help found and then head a foundation that makes major gifts to the San Diego community and teaches generations of women philanthropists. This was just the type of community involvement I craved, and the bonus was a whole new set of women

129

friends. Because of it, I also had the opportunity to learn about San Diego's issues and needs; and when the newly-elected Mayor assembled his staff, I had the background to be of assistance. Yes, I've gone back to work full time but in a job that allows me to make a community contribution. I've had to hire a driver for my seventh grader's after school activities and a dog walker. My fingernails are chipped and I've given up Pilates. But this is my choice for now. In my dreams, I've found a satisfying part-time job; but I'm guessing it will remain a dream. I continue to tell my children they are my highest priority, and we travel as a family to memorable spots that tie us together. But, it remains the great struggle balancing work and family, except now I know I can work full time and raise happy, productive children.

B.A., Mt. Holyoke College, J.D., with honors, Case Western Reserve. Julie Dubick was a U.S. Justice Department litigator and later general counsel and associate director of the U.S. Marshals Service. She was senior partner, now retired, at Seltzer Kaplan Wilkins & McMahon. She was a founder and past president of the San Diego Women's Foundation. She raised three happy, productive children while working full time. She is currently Director of Public Policy for San Diego Mayor Jerry Sanders.

Road Less Traveled

Sara L. May

I was never one of those people who always knew I was going to become a lawyer. I had exposure to the legal field: my father was a sole practitioner, and I worked in his office from the time I was ten years old. But, that notwithstanding, I had no real idea what career lay ahead. I have always been envious of those who have known, seemingly from birth, what career beckoned. I believed, however, that success lay with being happy in the choices one makes.

My career choice was not apparent to me. However, there was one thing I have always known: I did not want to have children. I have always known I was not going to have children. I had only one doll, a Floyd Little Doll (who was, at the time, the running back for the Denver Broncos). I babysat only once, and that was only as a result of extreme pressure from my mother and the desperate mother of the children in question. It was not an experience I chose to repeat. Simply, it is something I have always known and have never questioned.

People often wonder why I have made that choice. I don't usually explain – it isn't anyone's business. However, when I try, it is not something easily put into words. It is something I know. Is it a selfish decision? Perhaps. My husband and I have more freedom

131

than our friends who have children. Perhaps it is selfless – a child should be wanted by his or her parent. Perhaps it is somewhere in between. Perhaps it is something that need not be defended; it simply is.

Regardless, being child free is still not something easily accepted by society, even though many people have made that choice. It is not an easy choice for a woman to make, since it defies convention. I am fortunate that my friends and family have been accepting for the most part, if not entirely understanding. However, long ago I lost track of the number of people who told me I would change my mind, either when I reached some magical age, typically thirty, and the infamous biological clock began ticking, or when I met the right man. For the record, I did not change my mind, either when I reached thirty or when I met the right man. Dating proved to be equally challenging; it turned out that many men in their thirties had biological clocks that were ringing loud and clear. Societal pressure is not something to be underestimated.

Although I have long been clear about my personal goals, how I was going to make a living was not so clear. After graduating high school, I attended Colorado State University for one year. The school was not a good fit for me. I returned to Denver, unsure of my next step.

I spent that summer working at an Army/Navy surplus store. At the end of the summer, I did not necessarily know what I wanted to do, but I knew, without a doubt, that I did not want to continue selling fishing lures and hunting licenses! I eventually enrolled at the Denver campus of the University of Colorado. I went to school part time and worked full time for the Denver Center Theatre Company as the house manager. I enjoyed both. The Denver campus had small classes where lively discussions were the norm; the theatre company provided the opportunity to indulge my love of, and be part of, the performing arts.

The decision to go to law school occurred following a major management turnover at the theatre company. The new management wanted me to, in essence, double my workload, with

132

no corresponding increase in salary. This did not strike me as a good deal, and I quit.

I spoke to my college counselor and learned I could graduate in one year by taking eighteen units per semester. I knew that was feasible, but the large question loomed – what on earth was I going to do with myself after I graduated? I had not really focused on my future while in college. I was getting a degree in European history and political science. I also knew quite a good deal about theater management. However, none of these things led to any career that appealed to me.

I decided, in the absence of any other immediately apparent option, to take the LSAT exam and see where that led me. I did so with some hesitation because my parents had been doing their best to talk me out of becoming a lawyer. However, because I had been surrounded by the profession my entire life, I, unlike many who entered law school because they did not know what else to do, had a pretty good understanding of what the practice of law entailed.

I ended up at California Western School of Law, in part because I concluded there were worse things than to spend three years of my life in San Diego, California. Despite my initial ambivalence about taking the LSAT and embarking on a legal career, I was very happy in law school. It appealed to the scholar in me. I indulged in just being a student and excelling at only that, something I had not had the opportunity or luxury to do in college. I was a teaching assistant in the research and writing class, tutored, was on Law Review, and competed on a moot court team. I graduated magna cum laude.

With graduation looming, I was again, however, confronted with the dilemma of what to do with my life. I was fairly confident that being a trial attorney and working for a large law firm did not suit my personality. I thought my future lay in appellate law but did not know how to pursue that goal. For lack of any other clear path, I returned to Colorado and clerked, first for a state trial court and then for the Colorado Court of Appeals. I enjoyed both positions. I worked for two great judges, learned a great deal, and got to exercise my research and writing skills. It was an opportunity to learn about the law without the confrontation that seemed to go along with the practice of law.

A year after I returned to Denver, an enormous snowstorm occurred: the schools closed, and the snow damaged eighty percent of the trees. It led me to question why I had returned. With no immediately apparent answers, I began looking to return to San Diego. After some searching, I ended up at a major law firm, in the labor and employment group. Although this went against all the instincts I had about what suited me, I took the position, more concerned about escaping the snow and freezing temperatures than what was really good for me.

My original instincts that I was not meant to be a trial attorney were confirmed. Although I enjoyed the researching and writing, I loathed the discovery process and did not enjoy interacting with opposing counsel, all of whom, it appeared, had gotten a minor in law school in yelling. I was working eighty or ninety hours a week. I had bought a condominium and gotten a dog but felt I saw neither nearly enough. I made time to go horseback riding once a week but, more than once, ended up in the office after riding, still wearing my paddock boots.

I spent almost three years at the law firm. Although it wasn't a career that suited me, I do not regret my time spent at the firm. I made good friends and learned a great deal about trial and appellate practice as well as employment law. I had made enough money to buy a condominium, which subsequently led to being able to own a house outright before I turned forty. I also met the person who would, years later, introduce me to my husband.

Toward the end of my time at the law firm, half the labor and employment group left to form a new law firm. I was invited to go with them but declined, knowing that working for a start-up law firm was not the right decision for me. This decision was not easily made, since there was no telling what would become of my practice (because I had been doing the vast majority of my work for the client that was going with the new firm).

134

As it turned out, my practice was left in a strange and fragmented state. I was doing some transactional employment work, some litigation, and was defending a corporate client in a white-collar criminal proceeding. I was working on some appeals, which was what I liked to do, but realized I was never going to be able to do appellate work full time. It seemed the time had come to look elsewhere.

Not long after I began my search, I saw an opening for a central staff attorney at the California Court of Appeal. I applied and eventually got the job. The court was a revelation. I was no longer working eighty to ninety hour weeks. I had time to ride my horse, play with my dog, and volunteer at the San Diego Humane Society. For the first time in three years, I was not waking up in the middle of the night wondering if I had completed all the tasks for the previous day or making lists about the tasks I had to complete when I went into the office. More importantly, I really liked doing what I was doing. I could simply be a scholar, figuring out the right answer to often very complicated problems. I was doing nothing but researching and writing, and that satisfied my soul.

The court provided one more very interesting revelation. For the first time in my professional career, either as an attorney or otherwise, I was surrounded by other women who had chosen not to have children. Because I have always known I was not going to have children and have experienced significant societal pressure to do otherwise, it was very affirming to find myself working with so many others who had made that choice. This was particularly true because the courts are perceived to be places people choose to work because they are child friendly environments, with flexible and reasonable hours. The women at the court did not need to prove themselves by being the best trial lawyers, billing hundreds of hours each month. They were not striving to be superwomen – striving to be the best attorney at their firm and the best mom on the block – they, like me, simply enjoyed working to live, not living to work. They, like me, wanted to have a career they enjoyed that provided an intellectual challenge, but also allowed time for outside activities.

I spent six happy years at the court. I learned a great deal professionally and greatly improved my research and writing skills. I was able to be a scholar and to find solutions for complicated problems. I volunteered weekly at the Humane Society and learned how to train dogs. I pursued many different hobbies, unhampered by lengthy work hours. I met the man I would marry.

The time had come, however, to return to Denver, notwithstanding the snow. My parents were getting older; my husband was not happy at his job; and we concluded that even with the equity we had in the condominium, we were never going to be able to afford a house in the San Diego housing market. I returned to the Colorado Court of Appeals, this time on the central staff. And again, much to my surprise, I found myself surrounded by people, men and women, who have chosen to be child free. They have chosen a non-traditional job and not to have children. And they, like me, are very happy with their choices – personal and professional.

At the court, I continue to improve my research and writing skills and work on interesting cases. I stretch my brain every day. I play with my dog and have dates with my husband. I've started swimming and doing Pilates. I enjoy my hobbies and spending time with friends and family. It is, for me, the best place to be, at least for the moment.

The moral of the story? Be true to yourself. If you don't want children – don't have them. If you don't want to work in a law firm – don't. Understand what makes you happy and make choices accordingly. Don't shackle yourself to decisions you know aren't right simply because society states they are "what should be done." You don't need to become a partner in a law firm simply because that is the path your classmates have chosen. You don't need to have children because your friends are having them and your parents are yearning for grandchildren.

I have taken a different road. I didn't go to a traditional college. I didn't stay on the partner track. I didn't have children. I am, however, very happy with the decisions I have made and the road I am on. And, really, there's nothing more to want in life.

Sara May is an associate staff attorney at the Colorado Court of Appeals in Denver. She was a senior research attorney at the Fourth District Court of Appeal, Division One, in San Diego for six years and, prior to that, an associate in the labor and employment group at Gray Cary Ware & Freidenrich (now, DLA Piper US LLP) in San Diego. She served judicial clerkships at the Colorado Court of Appeals and at the trial court in Colorado's First Judicial District. She graduated magna cum laude from California Western School of Law and the University of Colorado at Denver. She lives in Highlands Ranch, Colorado, with her husband Daren. She enjoys playing with her dog, working out, and watching sports.

Tenure at Sixty

Jacquelyn H. Slotkin

I intended to follow in my father's footsteps: become a surgeon, get married, have a family. I would never have believed I would give up medicine for marriage. I am now sixty-five and would change few of my life choices (well, maybe my decision in 1960 to switch majors from pre-med to English after my boyfriend convinced me both of us could not be physicians if we wanted a family). My decisions about marriage, children, and career obviously predated the influence of the contraceptive revolution following the introduction of the first birth control pill in 1960.

Married for almost forty-five years and with three "planned" children (and now five grandchildren), I have been a life-long working wife and mother. I worked as a librarian, research analyst for a group of professors, cytology lab technician, secretary (thank goodness I listened to my mother and took that semester of high school typing), and substitute teacher. I have taught English in middle school, high school, and college. For six years, I was a practicing civil litigator. I have been a community volunteer and served on nonprofit boards. I am not nor have I ever considered myself a superwoman. This is my story about how I have balanced the demands – and the joys and satisfactions and crises and disappointments – of work and family.

I have earned a long list of educational credentials: a B.A., an M.A., (and Mrs.) in my early twenties; a Ph.D. in my thirties; and a J.D. at forty. At various times in my life, I've barely kept my foot wedged in the professional door while helping with homework assignments and science projects, introducing a huge king snake and hairy tarantula to my child's sixth-grade class, scheduling and driving carpools, coaching my daughters' soccer teams, observing my teenagers' tennis tournaments and gymnastics competitions, and teaching all my teenagers to drive. I've had my frustrations with parenting: a hyperactive son (before the diagnostic labels ADD and ADHD), one daughter with serious adolescent weight issues, and my youngest daughter with an over 4.0 GPA who wanted only to be a cheerleader.

My professional resume has "holes" because I never stopped being a nurturing mother and loving wife while continuing my education and employment. Interruptions and readjustments were necessary because of multiple moves for my husband's medical training and military service. In graduate school, my two-year-old daughter shared my library carrel for a year while I researched and wrote my dissertation. It was crammed with her books, toys, and blanket and with my stacks of books, note cards, and typewriter. In law school, my children studied with me in the law library every afternoon while I prepared for classes. My husband joined us for dinner in the law school's deli, and then took over homework and parenting in the evenings. When I practiced law, my children were responsible, once a month, for updating codes and loose-leaf services in our firm law library and copying documents (my youngest was the only one who could figure out how to copy two-sided court documents – obviously before state-of-the-art copy machines). Dinnertime conversation during law school was filled with discussions of interesting torts and criminal law cases and legal hypotheticals. (Later, my youngest daughter, who had developed an interest in the law, helped me to draft hypotheticals for my law students.)

140

In the early 1980s, the legal profession was not the most enlightened workplace for women. After taking the bar exam, I volunteered at Legal Aid while searching for a job. I was rejected by a medical malpractice defense firm because the male partner interviewing me explained they were looking for young men who would stay with the firm for their working lives (where was I going?). I wanted a job in the public sector where I had been volunteering and was told I was "a doctor's wife" and didn't "really need a job." I accepted an offer at a four-person firm. As a forty-year-old woman with a head of white hair, I was shocked when one of my favorite judges, after an ex parte hearing in chambers, swatted my "tush" with a file folder as I left his office. Imagine if that happened today! During a law and motion hearing on a psychological malpractice case where a treating psychologist had a sexual relationship with his patient, the judge, in sustaining the demurrer, announced he could not understand any argument about breach of fiduciary duty and unethical behavior because this was obviously "consensual sex among consenting adults." Two demurrers later, the case moved forward only because a new judge listened to my argument.

To quote a student of mine, now wife, mother, deputy district attorney, and president of Lawyers Club of San Diego, working mothers "can do it all" – women can be successful professionals and have satisfying home lives, but it takes less sleep, multi-tasking, organizational skills, and good childcare. In my case, to "do it all" required not doing it all at the same time and a supportive and often helpful spouse. I have always made lists – and still make lists – every day. I anticipate deadlines and almost always do everything well ahead of time. I arrive on time and often early for dinner invitations. I have never been late for class. I even wrote my own obituary before a recruiting trip to the Orient (to save my children the trouble of doing the research). And I returned to teaching in order to have more flexibility to enjoy a quality of life while being a professional, wife, mother, and community volunteer.

All my children were at home. At forty-five, I was ready to retire from my busy litigation practice. My husband encouraged me to do whatever would make me happy. One evening after a particularly long day of depositions, I read an advertisement in the local legal newspaper for a legal skills instructor position. The job sounded like a perfect fit: it would combine my love of teaching, my educational and teaching background, and my interest in and passion for the law. It was a two-year, non-tenure-track position. It could have been a dead end job, but the timing felt right. One of my law school classmates was teaching at California Western. When she saw my resume in the stack of resumes, she told the program director to hire me "on the spot." I was interviewed and hired.

I was in love – with my students, with teaching legal research and writing, with the work environment, and with the flexibility to work at home (because someone needed to be home for repairs and plumbers, to pick up sick teenagers, and to participate in their after-school school activities). It was not a prestigious, power position – certainly not comparable to a law firm position – and the pay cut was dramatic after private practice. I had joined the "pink ghetto" of law school teaching. Though legal writing positions were usually filled with women lawyers at the time I took the job, the mix has changed in my nineteen years of teaching at California Western. I found daily professional satisfaction, great mentors (in particular, the program director, Barbara Cox, younger by more than a decade but with wisdom, patience, and experience beyond her years), good friends among faculty and staff, and a renewed passion and energy for work.

I was warned by various tenured faculty that teaching legal research and writing would never lead to anything more. After the initial two years, I received a two-year extension. After four years, I became co-director, then four years later director of the research and writing program. Although I was not on tenure track, I produced law review articles (one describing an academic support program I had created for at-risk law students; others focused on role conflict and women lawyers in San Diego, an extension of my Ph.D. dissertation about college educated women and role conflict). The educational environment encouraged and supported my

142

scholarship, helped me expand my administrative skills, and nurtured my creative teaching.

In 1998, the new dean asked me to develop a master's program for foreign lawyers. I had been a skills teacher and administrator for ten years, and this job presented new challenges: organizing a program plan for the American Bar Association; preparing a self study for the ABA; hosting an ABA site visit to gain program acquiescence (approval); designing a U.S. law course and a legal research and writing course for foreign lawyers; and creating appealing program brochures, applications, recruiting materials, and web site. I also had to find students who wanted to live and to study in San Diego. I traveled to Brazil, Argentina, Chile, England, Germany, Vietnam, China, and Thailand with my computer and PowerPoint presentations. I wrote letters to international law school deans, law firms, and educational advisors. And the students arrived. The program has been an educational and financial success with more than 220 lawyers from forty countries participating and enriching the diversity of our law school community. I expanded my "Jewish mother" role to include my LL.M. students in my family's life. They have been invited to join our family for Thanksgiving every year. We host dinners and parties to celebrate their graduations. Even my cooking has improved!

And, in 2002, at the age of sixty, the faculty granted me tenure based upon my many years of teaching, scholarship, program administration, and law school service. Tenure feels like partnership in a big firm, but without the billable hours' requirement. Though I have never accepted the position as recording secretary for any organization, I find myself taking minutes at monthly faculty executive committee meetings as the newest – though certainly not the youngest – member of the tenured faculty.

I could never have done everything I've accomplished without my supportive spouse – the same man who convinced me to give up pre-med in college. The dean introduces him as an honorary member of the faculty because he attends many of my law school functions. I feel I have done it all – wife, mother, lawyer, volunteer, and teacher – using a more balanced, flexible standard. I have learned so much in my sixty-five years: some decisions are irreparable. You cannot give away your children or tell someone else to take the minutes! Some decisions are reparable: you can change jobs, professions, partners or spouses. You can make the decision to have a child or not have a child. My life has been productive and fulfilling. Confucius said it best: "If you enjoy what you do, you'll never work another day in your life."

B.A., University of Pittsburgh, M.A., West Virginia University, Ph.D., University of Arizona, J.D., University of San Diego. Jacquelyn Slotkin is a former legal research and writing professor and the Legal Skills Program director at California Western School of Law. Currently, she is the director of the LL.M./M.C.L. program for foreign lawyers at California Western School of Law – and, a tenured professor.

You Can Do It All

Lisa S. Weinreb

As a little girl, my parents instilled in me a sense of independence, determination, drive, and pride. My parents told me that a woman must be independent and be able to support herself. I was eight years old at the time and really didn't understand what they were trying to teach me. I remember one conversation in particular with my father when I was nine. My father told me I was expected to go to college and then to graduate school and become a "professional." Not really knowing what a professional was, I asked him if a go-go dancer was a professional since I already had these wonderful white go-go boots I wore every day! (Of course I had no idea what a go-go dancer was other than someone who got to wear cool boots.) He very kindly told me "no, dear." I asked him, "What is a professional?" My father rattled off a litany of professions such as doctor, dentist, lawyer, President of the United States. I settled on one just to get him off my back. "Okay. I will be a lawyer. Can I go play now?" That was the beginning of my trek to becoming an independent and ambitious attorney.

My father was a dentist, and my mother was a stay-at-home mom. As I grew older, they both continued to instill that sense of independence in me. They made sure I understood that I could do anything I wanted to do in life and that I had the same opportunities and responsibilities as a man. I didn't realize that also meant I had to mow the lawn just like my brother. My father made sure that when I began to drive, I knew how to take care of my car. He made me learn how to change the tires, replace the headlights, and refill all fluids (even though we had Triple A). My parents wanted to make sure I was empowered with the knowledge and skill to do things even if I didn't <u>have</u> to do them.

Those were very powerful lifelong lessons. I appreciate every one of them today. Growing up with that strong sense of strength and independence, I came to understand that I could do anything and everything I set my mind to.

I did go to college, I got married, I went to law school, and ultimately I became a Deputy District Attorney in San Diego. After many years of trying cases in the DA's office, I was assigned to the Gang Prosecution Unit. I try primarily murder and attempted murder cases committed by gang members. I love my job, but I also wanted to be active in the state and local bar associations. I became active in the San Diego County Bar Association, the California State Bar Association, and the Lawyers Club of San Diego, a local woman's bar association. I ultimately became president of that wonderful organization. I still wanted to do more. I taught trial advocacy as an adjunct law professor at California Western School of Law, mentored new lawyers and law students, taught trial advocacy for the National Institute of Trial Advocacy (NITA), for the National College of District Attorneys (NDAA), and for the California District Attorneys Association (CDAA). I was doing everything I wanted to do. And, during this time, I had two beautiful and wonderful children. Having children threw an entirely different challenge into the mix. I kept asking myself: how much havoc could two little kids add to my life as a career trial attorney?

As the kids grew older, I continued my activities in the state and local bar associations; but my life became more difficult to balance than I had ever anticipated. I was used to doing a lot of things and doing them well. I wasn't used to feeling completely inadequate in my responsibilities. My sense of inadequacy would rear its ugly head when I would drop my children off at school in my suit while the other moms were in their work-out outfits on their way to the gym. As I was prying my daughter off my leg to get her into the classroom so I could race to court on time, other moms were patiently waiting to volunteer in the classroom. So what did I do to alleviate the feeling of guilt I began to feel? I began to volunteer just like the other moms did. I agreed to be the room parent and organize field trips and class parties; I volunteered to be the team mom for my son's little league baseball team. I even volunteered to bake gingerbread cookies for my children's holiday parties in school. (Big mistake!)

As my responsibilities mounted as a Deputy District Attorney, President of the Lawyers Club, and mother, I was absolutely losing my mind. I began to have doubts about my ability to do it all. Could I really do everything? Could I actually have the career I have worked so hard for and be a good wife and mother to my children? To find the answer, I began reading books about how to balance career with family, but I was completely dissatisfied with the ending of them all. All of the stories would end up the same way. The woman would quit her job and end up staying at home. The final conclusion was that she couldn't do both. Well, I just wouldn't accept that; that was not how my story would turn out. I wanted to continue to work, I wanted to continue to be involved in the legal community, and I wanted to be an involved mother.

While there were days I doubted myself and doubted everything my parents had taught me, I ultimately came to the following conclusion: Yes, I can do it all. I can do it all and do it well!

However, there are a few things you must know and understand in order to be able to do it all and keep your sanity at the same time. First, you have to work harder and more efficiently than everyone else. You have more things to do than the average Joe, and you must cram it into the same twenty-four hours everyone else has. As a result, you will get much less sleep since you will have to use your normal sleep hours to finish everything you have to do during the day.

Second, you must have your spouse or significant other take on 50% of the workload at home. You must not and cannot accept any less. Simply because you are the women doesn't mean you have to do more work at home than anyone else.

Third, you will still feel inadequate no matter what you do. You will always feel like you could have done more for your children, you could have been a better spouse or partner, you could have done a better job on a brief, you could have gone to the gym to work out, and the list goes on. Just remember, every woman believes she could always do better. It is okay to bring store bought cupcakes to your daughter's class party instead of making them yourself. You simply don't have the time, and they will look and taste better than the ones you could have made anyway.

Four, the grass is always greener on the other side. Stay-at-home moms say to me, "It must be so nice to get dressed up every day and go to work." You see, they understand that when we get to work, we can have a cup of coffee, have a phone conversation, and go to the bathroom – all without being interrupted by a child during the day. It is actually a pretty good deal for us. Remember, stay-at-home moms are changing diapers, running carpools, doing laundry, putting away toys, and going to the grocery store. They are not having lunch and playing tennis all day.

I guarantee that even stay-at-home moms will say they wish they had spent more time with their children when they were young. Our children will grow up well adjusted and confident; they can do anything they want to do. They will understand that women can do all the things men can do because you have been a perfect role model for them.

And finally, take time for yourself. If you don't, you will burn out. Do not feel guilty if you need to get away for the weekend with your girlfriends or even leave town for a full week. I didn't heed this advice so well at first, and I was about to crack. At the last minute, I booked a flight to Mexico and stayed there for a week just hiking

148

and exploring remote villages. It was a week away I desperately needed. I no longer wait for that breaking point. I make sure I take trips and do things for myself so I can continue to do all the things I want to do in my life. I know you will feel like you should be spending the time with your children since you have been at work all day, but you will be no good to them stressed out and cranky. Taking time to do something for you is the most important aspect of being able to do it all. If you don't take care of yourself, you can't keep up the rigorous pace of your life. You don't have a choice here. If you want to do it all, you must take care of yourself.

Doing it all is a choice. It is not an easy choice, but it is possible. I know many people have written about why women can't do it all, but they are wrong. Many women have fought long and hard for us to have the ability to choose different paths in our lives. This is one of them. It is a choice we are fortunate to have, but it isn't a choice for everyone, only for those brave few. If you are going to work full time, be an involved mother to your children. Continue to be involved in organizations you are committed to. Once you have accepted the realities of what is in store, you will thrive. You will do it all, and you will do it all well!

We Can Do It All!
We can
be successful lawyers
and be wonderful parents
to our children
or caregivers to a loved one.
We can
be successful rainmakers
in our law firms
and be successful
wives, husbands, or partners.
We can
be successful leaders
in the legal community

and lead a well balanced
home life.
Don't let anyone tell you
that it can't be done.
We can do it all!

B.A., University of Texas, J.D., with honors, California Western School of Law. Lisa Weinreb has been a San Diego County Deputy District Attorney since 1995 (currently with the gang prosecution division). She serves as president of the Lawyers Club of San Diego. She has acted on the NBC dramamentary, Crime & Punishment. In addition, Lisa serves on the Board of Directors of the San Diego County Bar Association, Crime Victims United, and the San Diego County Bar Foundation. She is an adjunct professor of Trial Advocacy at California Western School of Law.